THE BOOK OF PURPOSE

The *You* Testament

Discover Your Purpose And Live It!

Tracy McNeil

TracyMac Publishing
A Division of Peace Place LLC
P.O. Box 767
Knightdale, North Carolina 27545

The author of this book does not offer medical advice or prescribe the use of any technique as a form of treatment for physical or mental problems without the advice of a physician, either directly or indirectly. The information in the book reflects a portion of the author's spiritual life and life experiences and is not intended to replace professional medical or psychological advice. The intent of the author is to assist you on your journey of discovery for spiritual well-being. In the event you use any of this information for yourself, the author and publisher assume no responsibility for you actions.

References:
Page 83, italicized text taken from http://www.marines.com/history-heritage/traditions
Page 144, italicized text taken from http://www.mayoclinic.com/health/meditation/HQ01070

Interior Design: TWA Solutions (www.twasolutions.com)

Cover Design: Owen McNeil – Another McNeil Creation

Cover Photography and Layout: Kea Taylor (www.imaginephotographyonline.com)

Dust Jacket Layout and Cover Revisions by TWA Solutions (www.twasolutions.com)

978-0-9891013-0-1 (Hardcover)
978-0-9891013-1-8 (Paperback)
978-0-9891013-2-5 (eBook)

Library of Congress Control Number: 2013907487

McNeil, Tracy A.
The book of purpose: the you testament / Tracy A. McNeil
First Edition

Printed in the United States of America

Table of Contents

Introduction: The Book of Purpose.................................7

Chapter One: Questions and Answers 13

It's Time.. 17

The Shower You 20

Me, Too 21

Smh @ Fear... 23

Chapter Two: The YOU Testament........................... 25

Write it Down.. 29

Interact.. 31

Accountability... 31

Chapter Three: What is Purpose?.............................. 33

Purpose, Mission and Passion................................ 42

Why and What Do I Need to Know?...................... 49

Chapter Four: Possible Hindrances of Discovery.............. 65

You 67

Stuck on repeat? 69

Self-disobedience... 72

Tradition 80

Beliefs.. 91

Blame 95

Procrastination... 101

Entertainment.. 105

Chapter Five: What is Your Purpose?....................... 115

Your Purpose... 117

From One Purpose to Another.............................. 119

Labels 127

Chapter Six: It's Your Turn!.. 131

    On Your Mark 133

    Get Ready.. 134

        Be Truthful 136

        Be Still 139

        Relax 141

        Pray 142

        Meditate 144

    Get Set.. 146

        Be Free 147

        Acceptance 148

    Let's Go! 150

Chapter Seven: Benefits of Discovery.............................. 157

    Discover.. 159

        Self-discovery 159

    Evolve 170

        Decisions... 171

        Change.. 177

        Growth.. 179

    Create 183

    Implement.. 189

    Achieve 192

Acknowledgments.. 197

About the Author.. 199

Dedication

This book is dedicated to Ambassadors for Christ Fellowship Center, Inc., established in 1982 in Havelock and home of MCAS Cherry Point, North Carolina, and founded by my parents, Walter E. Jones Sr. and Thomasine Rawls Jones, through 2007. It's where I grew with my siblings, Portia Smart and Walter Jr., and married my husband, Owen, in 1993. It's a special place that birthed so many life-changing experiences that became principles to live by and will always be close to my heart. Ambassadors is where I learned to go beyond the ceiling and the four walls with God, enjoyed some of my best relationships and friendships ever with people who now live all over the world and it's where my journey of self-discovery began! It was purposed to be a ministry of hope and reconciliation and a training ground. For me, and thousands of others, it was indeed! I am truly grateful. May all our lives forever teach and sing, "Let There Be Love..."

Introduction

THE BOOK OF PURPOSE

THE BOOK OF PURPOSE

It's trendy to hear people talk about things like purpose, destiny, consciousness, awakening, passion, mission and vision. Is it just a trend? Do you ever wonder what it all means and if anything, what does it have to do with you? Sometimes hearing those conversations in or outside your mind has an effect that can go from awe-inspiring to outright confusing as hell! The explanations can be soul stirring or head scratching. Once all the voices go silent, some may experience a form of betterment and others are left soul scratching and head stirring. Tired of the deep, philosophical hoopla they are still left wanting the simplicity of purpose. Purpose is serious business, but it is *everything* that should make you happy. Absolutely! So many people are seeking peace, happiness or meaning through spiritual teachings and conversations because they have come to a place in life that what they are experiencing is void of satisfaction and just not good enough anymore. It's like your foot itching when you have on a sock and a boot, you just can't scratch it. Others are introduced to the world of purpose because they want a change or they are going through a transition that ordered a wake-up call. We transition from conception all the way to decomposition and maybe even beyond. So not all transitions are negative, but they do serve a purpose.

Transitions are those times when something is expiring and another is being birthed. Both are unfamiliar, but sure occurrences and life is full of those moments. Transitions can be minor and have a very subtle effect on your life. Like transitioning to another size shoe is subtle unless you've got newsworthy feet! Others can be evolutionary, extremely life changing and leave no semblance of life as you knew it. Transitions can be having a child, buying a new car, divorce, starting a business, returning from war, starting school, bankruptcy, an empty nest, promotion, building your dream home, losing a loved one, rekindling a relationship, military deployment, a merger, winning a settlement, graduating, a geographical move, illness, a milestone birthday, a prognosis, caring for an elderly loved one, a first or a last. See, not all transition is negative, but it can be such a delicate time since letting go of one thing and reaching for the other creates a moment where you don't have a good grip on either. Sometimes transition can bring peace or spark fear and uncertainty that bring on big questions you don't have the answers to. Why is this happening to me? What am I going to do? Will I make it? What does this mean? Where is God in this? How can I get out of this? What should I do? Why didn't I see that coming?

You want answers. You want to know the reason and the *purpose* for the situation. You want practical solutions.

All of the questions that are birthed out of transition deserve answers and all of those answers can create the best possible solutions for your life. Transition can create the best opportunity to answer those questions by discovering more than just the purpose behind the situation, but also discovering *your* purpose. Purpose has a way of revealing answers and solutions that bring peace to your entire life, not only to one particular crisis at hand. You may think some of those situations can be solved with a little more money, and that may be true, but for how long? You may have had those money matters before and that money came and went as if your pocket was a revolving door. Now what? You may feel the situation would be different because of what he/she did or didn't do, but it happened! Now what?

Transition can be the stimulus for self-discovery and how to have more meaning in your life by understanding who you are because everything you have or have not experienced serves a purpose—your purpose. You deserve to know what that is, thus it is your privilege and responsibility. You want to know why you're here so your life can have meaning. You want to know the right questions to ask and receive the best answers, results and solutions. You don't want mind-blowing philosophy. You want peace of mind. And, you'd like that to happen quickly and be as simple as possible. With your best effort, you've probably already tried. You may have reached out before and the answers did not satisfy your questions. You may have reached out, found some temporary relief in activity, and got tired of it or developed a habit that eventually enslaved you to it. You may have reached out to your profession, but even being at the top of your game or just glad to be on the bench, the satisfaction of monetary wealth alone is not paying your mind. You may have accepted religion only to feel rejected because of it not being what you thought it would help you to become. You may reach out to an extravagant lifestyle of material possessions only to find the clothes you buy only feed your closet because your life is still hungry with nothing to wear—no place to be—and even the latest trend seems to age in dog years. You may not have ever reached out at all or maybe your efforts have been quite fulfilling thus far. Either way, I applaud you since you reached for this book, which will not disappoint. It means you're asking questions and for some reason you just know there are answers.

Chapter One

QUESTIONS & ANSWERS

QUESTIONS & ANSWERS

❦

You are reading this book because you want to know something. In this case, you want to know about your purpose and life's mission and if you already know it, you want to know more. This is not a new set of values or beliefs, nor am I trying to get you to agree with me about anything. It is an opportunity for you to agree with yourself. An internal and external agreement that gives you peace of mind to reveal what you already know. The purpose of this book is to (1) Help you *discover* who you are, (2) *Evolve* within your purpose, (3) *Create* advancements for your life's mission(s), (4) *Implement* the principles you develop with passion to serve the greater good and (5) *Achieve* creating the foundational resource for you to live by—the YOU Testament. And, if nothing else, it will at least cause you to think or re-think about some things in a different light. It is also a stimulus for you to create purposeful questions and answers. This is a resource to help you appreciate your spiritual self and to realize who you are, value your beliefs and live a life full of peace, wisdom, success and abundance with passion.

Most questions don't come without answers following close behind. Even if the answers aren't complete, be sure they are forming and maturing. In order to understand something, including ourselves, we can't be afraid to ask questions, especially about purpose, mission and passion. One of the best ways to develop an understanding of anything, including purpose, is to ask questions. Questions asked reveal your intelligence and answers become so proud, they want you to have them. If you are afraid or just too cool to ask questions, the answers feel the same way about you. Let's decide to ask some questions and trust that reading this book and doing the work of purpose will be a conduit to reveal the solutions tailored for your life. Bring your whole self in and do the work! As that happens, and it will, the answers will come to the degree they can trust you to live them. You can't disappoint them: they are yours. This is your testament.

Most people have questions about their purpose, vision, mission and the meaning of their lives. Questions create answers. Some questions we all have may be: What is purpose? What is purpose versus mission and passion? Why should I know my purpose? What are some of the hindrances and benefits of knowing my purpose? How do I discover my purpose and carry out my mission? What is *my* purpose and why am I here? What do I do when I discover my purpose? How do I implement and make it practical? If you've ever asked any of these questions before, trust that when asking them now, the answers—YOUR answers—are here within YOU already! Yes!

Now, don't think of purposeful questions as daunting. This is a celebration! A spiritual spa relaxes your entire life. Feel good about it, be happy and smile—you have a purpose! It's not as if you will have a goofy, smile glued on twenty-four-seven, but *you can enjoy the power and the reality of consistent contentment.* Purposeful questions expose your spiritual intelligence so expect brilliant results. The questions have only seemed difficult because you have previously distanced yourself from them. Now draw them close and embrace them, they need you as much as you need their answers. Purposeful questions form when you are ready for the answers. You will discover some of your answers while reading this book. One single resource may never put *all* of your questions to rest. But, the purpose of this resource is to be a relevant solution for you as you discover yours, a solution so you can live in peace now and not wait to rest in it! What is so amazing about purpose is that every single person who reads this book and is asking the same questions will discover unique solutions that fulfill their own lives.

It's Time

Be it a trend, transition or curiosity, it's time to receive the answers and solutions you are looking for, as they are looking for you, too. That intersect is the beginning of self-discovery. The answers and solutions are ready. You will find out because this time your reach goes within. That may be a farther reach than the distant ones you've made externally. It's time to pull out all the stops, let go of the excuses you've used for years and enjoy life the way you were purposed to. This time you reached out and have found a resource to help you during your transition and assist you in discovering your purpose, execute your mission(s) and achieve with great passion. You have reached for self-help, been invited to ways to help yourself, and it's time to help yourself to your purpose!

I'll define purpose and other terms for the sake of reading continuity. The definitions offer a perspective, but the answers and interpretations will be all yours. Yet, *purpose* works anywhere, all the time and with anybody who will! Your interpretations will be as unique as your fingerprint, but the commonality will be discovering and knowing purpose and experiencing self-discovery. That will initiate a spiritually unified bond that will ultimately serve the infinite greater good. So get ready, be ready for answers in a way that will change your life for your own betterment and benefit the world, causing a rippling effect on purpose. Get ready to receive the answers and live them. Get ready to become an answer. Get ready to do the work, but don't fear the process for in purpose, work and play are friends that walk hand-in-hand. It's time!

Your Testament: How could I sabotage this process? What will I do to avoid doing those things?

_____

_____

_____

_____

_____

_____

_____

_____

_____

_____

_____

_____

_____

_____

_____

_____

_____

_____

_____

_____

_____

_____

_____

_____

The Shower You

Your life may be filled with questions that may sometimes leave you feeling there is no livable answer, at least not practical enough for you to be consistent. Discovering your purpose through transition or curiosity can develop the spiritual and mental stamina it takes to ask the questions and receive the best answers, whether difficult or not. You want solutions that make sense and outweigh the problems. As we journey in self-discovery, the questions and answers aren't flippantly coming from the surface person who everyone sees, but the essence or spirit of who you are, the *shower you*. The *shower you* is who you are by yourself, without walls or external manipulation, relationship negotiations, the untouched; *where the level of income, accomplishments, education, body type, social activity, marital status, demographics, position, relatives, the car you drive or don't, or the friends you have or won't have doesn't matter.* Who is that?

You may initially feel weak or lost without all of those layers, but this form of disrobing reveals the strength and purpose of who you really are. This is the essence of who you are; your purest self. When it all boils down, no matter how far you have reached out or who you've reached for, *what you really want is the reality of who you are to be the best you there is!* So don't think of the *shower you* as being stripped down to cause humiliation, look at it as being freed up from the responsibilities of titles, functions and social labeling to just be! There is a huge difference between being stripped and you stripping. This is a shift in consciousness you willingly make. It is an amazing opportunity to be free and become pleased with who you see. The *shower you* is the one who combines all the wisdom from every past and current experience, the dreamer of future endeavors, who makes a conscious decision to be one with all things divine and universal, and the one who not only lives robustly in the power of now, but also defines it. This reflection is the *you* who was designed for purpose in the image and likeness of God. The *shower you* is your most authentic self, physically naked, but spiritually clothed in divine purpose. It's the happiest you, the one who laughs the heartiest, the most beautiful, the most courageous, the most precise and excellent, the most giving, resilient, peaceful, inquisitive, intelligent, most talented and skilled, the strongest, most vibrant, wise, attractive, kind, hospitable, free and is not bound by thoughts of limitations. It is the best of you expressed through purpose. That *you* is the one who asks questions and builds a relationship with the answers to become a solution. This book is purposed exactly for the *shower you*. There are not two of you. The *shower you* is the only you there is. Anything else is the perception of a weak imposter. Purpose makes sure you don't get fooled!

Me, Too

I remember having so many questions about my life and just about everything else, due to just being curious and sometimes because of a variety of transitions. I was also skeptical of so many things and to some degree, I still can be. I didn't verbalize my questions too much, having to do with the way I was brought up. If I asked my mom how to spell a word, she'd say, "Try to look it up in the dictionary first." If I had a question about something in the Bible, my dad would say, "Always read it for yourself." What was up with those people? Don't get me wrong, they did help me understand so much about life and helped me learn how to take the initiative. I love and appreciate them for that. The discipline of having to find out for myself allowed me to research and reach out through religion, music, sometimes materialism and a few self-help books. I read different translations of the Bible, studied concordances and spiritual lessons. I read labels, instructions, directions for everything and I had it so bad I wouldn't listen to a new album, cassette tape or CD until I read *all* the liner notes. I even read my husband before I married him and the story of our relationship is still being written and it is turning out to be quite nice. Those resources helped me and made great contributions to my life, and I probably wouldn't be writing to you if it weren't for those resources, especially my parents and my husband. The pages of my daughter's life seem to turn way too fast, but I am so grateful to be present as they are written. She's one of the reasons why I stopped reading so many books and started reading life. I'm so grateful. But, just reading paper books and materials helped answer some of my questions, but the satisfaction didn't last long because I'd soon have another one.

"Okay, I got that, but what about…" Oh boy! The questions just kept coming, especially the ones about God. I loved my relationship with God, *the creative and all sustaining power, and connecting life source for all there is* and that two-way dialogue is what kept me wanting to know more and be more. I reached out by going to church just about every day and most nights of the week, and it still wasn't enough. I'd buy the trendiest clothes and shoes I liked; my shopping bags were full and I was still left wanting. I ordered the latest music and still felt like I was missing a beat. I didn't reach out for relationships often since people seemed to be preoccupied with their own issues and I didn't want to add to it. I would even read a few spiritual and self-help books that were inspiring. I did a lot of reading, some for knowledge, but a lot out of skepticism, but that's all it seemed to be, just reading. I should have been happy for the most part and had every reason to be very satisfied. But, I had this little nagging tug on my life that became so annoying, like that itch in the boot I mentioned earlier. I couldn't scratch it well enough. It kept presenting questions that my boxed life couldn't find the answers to, as if my questions were too big for the world I lived in and they kept tugging at me and kept calling me out. I had to take that boot and that sock off!

Smh @ Fear

I was scared. I didn't know where to go or what I would discover, especially if the journey led to nowhere. Although I was scared, fear wasn't as bold as those questions or as desperate as I was for practical answers. I didn't cast fear aside, I couldn't. But, I did not let it block the possibility of learning. I would eventually discover that being scared is a temporary sensation; an uncanny knack of imagination that can create stressful feelings, justified or not. It has the ability to completely ignore real-time evidence and use imagination for naught. So, I took fear with me—so I wouldn't be alone—to see if it had some questions. Come to find out, fear was scared, too. I just knew there was more to life than my current experiences. My physical and mental ruts were wearing a bald pattern in the creativity of mind. I knew there just had to be more to my existence than my mundane routines and one-track mind. I knew there just had to be more to my life. I knew there was more to me. I wanted to know who I was beyond reading and being labeled, fighting against stereotypes and expectations, my decorated box, clichés and my stuff (people, too). I wanted to know my purpose, mission and passion. It took some time for me to have the courage to listen to the answers and to begin to trust the solutions enough to live them. It was a slow start, but on February 27, 1990, my twenty-first birthday, I made a commitment to get to know me, who I was and I started the journey to discovering my purpose. The journey allowed me to travel within, but didn't take me far out. Part of my journey revealed that helping you discover your purpose and mission is one way I continue to advance my own. Do you know what else I discovered? Fear was an ignorant and weak companion. It ended up leaving every time I wouldn't give it my ideas, which resulted in it not having much to say.

Chapter Two

THE "YOU" TESTAMENT

THE "YOU" TESTAMENT

I offer you principles, accounts, share some of my real and practical experiences and parts of my testament of self-discovery. They have helped in my journey, my clients in theirs and I pray they will assist you with yours. A testament is valuable; it can be the deciding factor in a life-changing verdict. In the world of self-help material, there is usually not a lot of thinking space for the reader to be reflective or held accountable to make practical application. You already know a wealth of information about what others think and believe. But, what about you, what do YOU think? What do YOU believe? What do YOU know? How do you intertwine all of that and make sense of it all in a way it benefits your life for practical application, advancement and overall betterment? What is your testament? This is where you become accountable to the development of your testament and implement the relevant matters of your heart. Accountability can come from outside reinforcements, but it has to start with you. A life coach, speaker, counselor, spiritual advisor or author can offer strategic principles. They can give you "3 How To's," "The 10 Reasons to…" or all the tools necessary for betterment that can be explained thoroughly and laid out like a good, old fashioned *Ms. Celie's* breakfast. You may have those who can and want to help you, but they can't do the work for you and they can't want more for you than you want for yourself. You have to eat the breakfast *Shug*. They can make suggestions, but you have to decide to be accountable. You have to implement. Sometimes the implementation of new thoughts requires repetition. The intentional use of repetition is to provide a great opportunity for conditioning in self-discovery. There may be things you may not have thought about this way before or maybe your transition is allowing you to re-think some principles. And, like anything else you know for sure, it took more than one time to seal the deal. It is also to strategize, compete and win against the possible negativity you've had on repeat. What you repeat you are more likely to implement.

Implementation is the evidence of accountability and one of the simplest ways to begin implementation is to write it down. Whether it's a "to do" list, a grocery list, blueprints, a letter or a testament of your life, writing allows you to have mercy on your thoughts and keeps them from bullying you. It can bring a great deal of organization to help you implement those things that are worthy and disregard the ones that don't make the cut. Self-discovery is a continuum of implementation so writing can be instructional and memorable. You've read great books written about different things and people. Books some people find most sacred were written by those who were said to be inspired by God. They were fellow humans who wrote testaments, accounts and historical recollections about their perceptions of their lives and the lives of others. Allow God to inspire you, too. They were no different from you, right? Right!? What better way to stop being a stranger to who you are than to record the processes of your discovery? Even biographies and autobiographies about influential people required someone to write about what they discovered about themselves and others. Who better to write about you than you? And, what better time to write about who you are and are purposefully becoming than now?

Write It Down

Imagine how it would feel to get a handwritten note from someone you love, especially these days. An e-card, post on social media, email is okay, but a letter makes you feel special. Handwriting can resonate in a way that typing or texting may not do with some of us. It's a unique expression of your person. It requires you to slow down, be aware of what you are thinking, and be more conscious of how you convey it. Sometimes your thoughts go so much faster than your fingers you wonder who started the race. Your *You Testament* is like writing a letter to yourself, an account about your discovery and the experience becomes a personal treasure and a significant resource of your lifetime. Whenever you have new discoveries you can use your *You Testament* to be a reference of accountability for what to do and maybe lessons of what not to do. But, how you choose to compose your testament is ultimately up to you. I have provided writing space for your convenience, but if typing your *You Testament* is more fitting, so be it. I have used vocal recordings to chronicle parts of my journey and have even set some of them to music. I know handwriting may seem archaic and some is almost illegible. Some schools don't even teach children to write in cursive anymore. Your handwriting says something about you; after all, there are handwriting experts. I've never seen a writing expert interpret a font. I typed this book, and be glad I did. I write with my left hand (but do just about everything else with my right) and you may have thought it was a book of hieroglyphics or a very long prescription. But, typing was the result of decades of portions of my handwritten notes, journals, music, thoughts, diaries and quotes.

It will be so exciting to see your life evolve from discovering who you are by creating your testament. As you realize your purpose and missions, you will be developing the passion to achieve repeatedly! I'm so excited with you! So, you don't have to write and, of course, I can't make you, but write if you can. (If you do, I'll give you a sticker.) However you choose to record your purpose, unfolding is completely up to you, though, as you can see, writing is encouraged. But, your creativity and your tools are only limited by the assignments you give them. Document, however you choose, consistently and on purpose and it may not matter to you how you create your testament, but that you are interactive while doing the work and implementing the process.

Interact

Use your tools of implementation deliberately and consciously. Being interactive monitors your inner activity—what you are thinking without becoming lost in thought, how you are feeling without being overcome by emotion, what solutions are coming to mind and creating a plan for them, etc. Questions are throughout the book, so be aware and sensitive that self-discovery is happening since the *shower you* is already emerging in purpose and matures by being interactive. It knows we're talking about it and is a loved ONE already! That is who you want to hear from, the power you want to live from the place you want to love from.

Take your time and be patient with yourself as you answer the questions. Be open to create your own questions and answers for even more clarity. Your participation allows you to interact or transmit your thoughts and feelings to bring the awareness of who you are to your life. You can reap and experience the unlimited benefits of living purposefully and applying what you discover to every aspect of your life. Commit to use this interactive tool for practical application. Be truthful. You can't cheat on you and not know it. Besides, being interactive through self-discovery is not a game.

Accountability

It's been established that writing or some form of consistent recording is advantageous for implementation and accountability. It's a beginning. If you read something that's one thing, but when you write it, repeat and understand it, you are more likely to implement it. The lack of accountability can keep you from making the connection from what is heard or read and how to live it. So, the hearers and readers may have a positive experience for a moment, but are not quite sure how to connect helpful truths and principles with the functions of day-to-day life. Sometimes, it is due to laziness. It's okay to be lazy sometimes and it's not lethal to your existence, but it can be genocide to your dreams and goals. Transition and the initial implementation of discovery are too delicate for you to be lazy. Some people would rather lazily accept a socially assigned identity or, like a parasite, become solely dependent on the identity of another rather than do the work of self-discovery.

Chapter Three

WHAT IS PURPOSE?

WHAT IS PURPOSE?

Purpose means the reason for which anything is done, created or exists. Purpose can also be defined as aim, intention or goal. Anything created or designed without an intentional use or reason is automatically subject to abnormal or incorrect use. It doesn't matter if it's a pen or a book, if the intended desire or reason is not identified it is subjected to misuse or rendered useless. It would be ridiculous to try to turn pages on a pen or even more outlandish to write with a book because you know what they are and what they are supposed to do. You know the *purpose* of those things. They were designed for a specific and identifiable purpose. That's not saying they could never be used beyond the initial or intended purpose, but knowing what the purpose of those things are ensures premium function.

So, if we give things purpose, how much more imperative is it to know our own? Who are you? What is your purpose? When it comes to wanting to know or discover one's life purpose or the individual meaning of life, the questions posed are: What is my reason for being? What was I created to be? Ultimately, who am I? Purpose is your spiritual identity—the *who* that you are. Purpose identifies and illuminates the *shower you*, which is your purest essence that goes beyond your name, occupation, family, status and social ties—that intriguing character that everything worthy in your life is attracted to and loves being associated with! Purpose is who you are before being labeled, categorized, or shaped by opinion. There are people who say, "I know my purpose" and they immediately list a job title, education, social status, function, service, good deed or task. In no way am I discounting their information that may be factual and profitable. I humbly submit to you; that there is more to them than what they do. Yes, we all have missions and things we may be passionate about doing, but what you do is not who you are. Purpose being your spiritual identity, lives way beyond letters in your names, accomplishments, functions or duties. It gives meaning or definition to your tangible and intangible existence. It's the core reality of the essence of who you are and how you live.

The most significant aspect of purpose is that it is the expression of the attributes and characteristics of God through you. When I was a little girl, I remember thinking God was this big man that looked like one of the King Henrys or my original concept of Father Time. He sat on a huge, golden throne with light that shone through and around him so bright, you'd have to squint, as if you were looking directly into the sun, just to attempt to see a blinding silhouette. Of course, he wore a gold crown—Bedazzled, Bejeweled, and he had a gold scepter, too. I thought

God had a huge book that looked like my grandparents' family Bible that sat on the coffee table in their living room. You know the one that somebody started writing names, anniversaries and birthdays in and stopped somewhere around, umm...1973. It had old, black and white, blurred pictures of relatives I never knew, a lock of somebody's hair from a first haircut, an obituary or two, somebody's wedding or funeral flowers that had been pressed by the weight of the pages and a piece of somebody's Easter speech in it. And, though it was dusty, you better not touch it, much less read it. *What was I doing in their plastic covered living room anyway?* Yeah, I thought God had a big book like that, only gold without the dust and with a lot of writing in it. But, when I was old enough to have to listen during Sunday school, I specifically remember being taught that God was omnipresent, omnipotent and omniscient. I read it for myself, looked up those words in the dictionary and I believed it. So, that completely messed up my visual. It also shifted my relationship with God and birthed questions. I thought about it for a long time and concluded: If God was omnipresent, I could no longer limit God's location to my idea of heaven. There was nowhere God couldn't be, including in you and me. If God was omnipotent, I couldn't tie God to just my limited imagination because God had the power to be everywhere and do anything all the time. And, if God were omniscient, why would God need to write anything down in a book? God knows everything all the time! Now you see what I mean when I say I had questions too big for the world I lived in. But, I began to see and relate to God in a way that questioned my perception and went beyond my limits. I realized and believed: *God is the creative and all sustaining power and connecting life source for all there is. God is...* That is how I see God. That is how God is. That is who God is. That is enough!

Your Testament: What do I believe about God? How do I see God? How do I think God sees me?

_____

_____

_____

_____

_____

_____

_____

_____

_____

_____

_____

_____

_____

_____

_____

_____

_____

_____

_____

_____

What is Purpose?

How you see God and how you believe God sees you has a lot to do with how you see yourself, especially through the eyes of purpose. How you see yourself shapes how you view other people. Individually, we cannot adequately represent all the infinite attributes of such a magnificent Deity. But, each of us has a purpose identified by unique expression(s) and collectively, we are comprised of all God is. It reveals our connection to others and with ourselves. It is not about being some out of touch cream puff or a pushover because purpose doesn't discount aggression, anger, a *bad* attitude, unhappiness, displeasure, frustration, annoyance and the like. Purpose can use the wisdom of passion to deploy those traits as tools for your mission, but they won't control you. Purpose allows the reason for our original intent to emerge rather than projecting a self-image solely based on the possibly ignorant opinion of others. It helps you design your visions and live your best dreams wide-awake. Your purpose or spiritual identity provides an innate GPS; not only knowing why you are, where you are and how to navigate. Purpose is an inside job. It is not the path you walk out, but the identity you walk in. It is the priceless treasure you are here to be.

Your Testament: What do I believe about purpose?

_____

_____

_____

What is Purpose?

Purpose, Mission and Passion

Before we go any further, let's look at the difference between purpose, mission and passion. Some believe purpose, mission and passion are one and the same and that may be the truth of their experience. I really needed to see them separately, so I could more successfully understand, strategize and implement. No matter how great the purpose, plan or high the goals you have the responsibility to execute. It's torturous to think and re-think about your purpose and not give it an assignment or lack the energy to bring it to life. Seeing the difference between purpose, mission and passion could very well be the ticket to advance from thought to achievement! *Purpose is who you are and why you are here. Mission is what you are here to do and the means by which you function. Passion is the energy and level of intensity by which you successfully carry it out, consistently.* They are your why, what and how.

You can change your mission or complete it. Some missions automatically progress to another. Your profession or career path, social connectivity, functions, titles and duties are assignments that are subject to change. Therefore, since your assignments can be changed; it is dangerous to substitute them for purpose. You may be offered a job, you may earn a promotion, get laid off, fired or retire. They can come and go, but who you are is not controlled by your missions. That is why your missions may very well be many, but your purpose remains constant and you consciously bring who you are into everything you do. *I believe that purpose is who you are and why you are here, mission is the common thread of, and the means by which you*

42

carry out your purpose; the vehicle. Passion is the level of power of the emotion, willingness to sacrifice and boundless enthusiasm and intensity used to do it. The passion is the fuel. It's not always 100%. You have decisions to make, there are responsibilities to time, the cooperation of others, spiritual maturation, human limitations, needful rest and quiet and finances are just some of the things that can affect your mission and the intensity or your level of passion.

Your passion is turned on by purpose regardless of the mission. Passion will fuel the mission as long as purpose says so. Passion is in love with purpose no matter what the mission looks like. It's your spiritual heart rate. Passion is the personal trainer for each mission and keeps it in shape for purpose sake! It's what gives you the enthusiasm to make a career change in spite of opinion and the economy or the drive, go back to school to freshen up skills or develop a new talent for purpose. It is also the strength you need to sit down when stress says keep going, as well as the power to abandon fear by keeping your head up, eyes focused and mouth shut during a challenge. It's the zeal that establishes the exercise regimen for the mission. Passion is the driving force for having joy and being happy about your assignment and it gets the opportunity to demonstrate the work ethic of the *shower you*. It's energizing the most excellent you there is to do what comes natural and it is on fire, but not burned out! Being passionate is enjoying the mission, having the energy and intensity for it. Passion can show up for work even if the direct deposit has yet to make it to the bank because passion isn't in it just for the pay, it's in it for the pleasure. You love to do it and to be sure, it loves you too!

Your Testament: What was the last thing I was the most consistently passionate about? What is something I would do for free, for at least five hours per day, if all of my financial concerns were taken care of? Why that? How is that different from what I am doing now?

_____

_____

_____

_____

_____

_____

_____

_____

_____

_____

_____

_____

_____

_____

_____

_____

_____

_____

_____

_____

_____

_____

_____

What is Purpose?

If your purpose is to be peace, integrity, administration, wisdom, empowerment, freedom, courage, hope, love, abundance, etc., then your mission—how you carry out your attributes—will always benefit what you do. For instance, if peace and/or abundance are your purpose, then your mission will be what peace and abundance do—what job they take. Your purpose may be peace or abundance, but your mission(s) may be a teacher, IT specialist, actor, government employee, CEO of a company, fireman, chef, courier, manicurist, musician, dog trainer, a soldier, author, and so on. So peace or abundance is manifested and, as you function through those capacities, you advance your life's missions. You have a sense of belongingness and pride no matter what you do because what resonates is operating from the power of who you are. No matter what you do or where you go, peace and/or abundance enter the room when you show up! When you are making the bed, that's peace, when you are driving down the street, that's abundance, when you are washing your hands, peace is, too, when you are having a conversation, your lips belong to abundance, if you are making copies, peace is, too, when you are pushing a cart in the grocery store, abundance is you, if you are at a family reunion, peace has got to be there! Always know that being who you are is always…enough! Should you change the mode of transportation, the mission of your purpose or it gets changed by someone else or gets interrupted, all is well since you'd still be…peace, abundance, etc.! You are still who you are. If the company folds, you are still your purpose: peace and abundance or whatever divine attributes of God you are. If he/she walks away, who you are is not lost at all! When your children are grown, gone, and come back, or if friends change, you are still the resident expert of peace and abundance—they use your house, your body to reside in. In sickness and in health, for richer or poorer—your awakened purpose, peace and abundance will not be denied. You as peace, abundance, or the reason for your existence can express who you are through your missions. That's why titles and missions are not to be sought after first - they don't define you, they are too limited. You could be still (and sometimes you should) and be your purpose, although the integrity of your mission does require progression and implementation.

Your Testament: What attributes of God do I believe I express now? What am I thinking? Create questions and answers.

_____

_____

_____

_____

_____

_____

_____

_____

_____

Why and What Do I Need to Know?

There are probably people who go through life who don't give a flying flip about knowing their purpose or could not care less whether or not you discover yours. They go through life from day to day, seemingly satisfied. Some know their purpose and choose not to live it. In other cases, ignorance may be bliss. Because purpose, which is your spiritual identity, may not be something you *discover*, per se. It is what you realize, remember, develop and release. Why do you need to know? You really don't *have* to know anything you don't want to. It's a choice, and I've even heard some say it's a luxury. But, because you're still reading this book, you've revealed your curiosity and desire to know. Gotcha! The answers begin to be revealed in the desire to know. Knowing your purpose or mission is not a matter of life or death, but it has a great deal to do with *how* you live or die therefore it has everything to do with your overall quality of life, level of fulfillment and relationships. Remember, anything created, designed or exists without a purpose, reason or intent is subject to abnormal or improper use. If you don't know why you are here or what you are here to be and do, you are more likely to be used improperly, misunderstood, mistreated or even abused by others and yourself. The thing about it is if you're self-ignorant, you won't even recognize your victimization until it's done.

Look around the world and depending on your paradigm, you may see things very chaotic or have perceived evidence of an *end times* because of wars, human atrocities, hypocrisy, and extreme weather patterns, all of which can seem very dismal or even depressing.

You may see a spiritual awakening, greater connectivity, innovation and the opportunity for invention, change and solutions, which can be very hopeful and exciting. How you view people and the world has a whole lot to do with the condition of your vision, your spiritual eyes. Going around not being able to see clearly distorts your experience(s). Purpose can correct your vision and outlook.

Physically, I have big eyes and poor eyesight. What a combination! I should be able to see anything all the time, with these things. But, I've been wearing glasses since middle school. Well, I *should* have been wearing them since middle school. I had glasses, but the frames were so big they touched my eyebrows and my cheeks at the same time and they looked like flat-screen TVs. The lenses looked like they were made out of glass cinder block. They were so heavy I needed a kickstand to keep them from sliding down my face and the nose rests left little dark blemishes on the sides of my nose. This must have been a joke or an early method of birth control for any future possibilities. My eyes were so big and the lenses were so thick, I looked like a frog looking through ice! Remember the character Redd Foxx played in the movie *Harlem Nights*? Exactly!

The awkward age when middle school is already challenging, I was not going to add wearing a set of glass coasters to my drama. Since I didn't wear my glasses, as I should have, my vision worsened over time and started affecting me in other ways. My grades slipped because I couldn't see the blackboard. I didn't move to the front of the class, I thought the front of the class was for those who did front-of-the-class work. The writing on the blackboard was distorted. No, it was my eyes. I squinted so much I almost started developing crow's feet at twelve. In high school, I was the only one in my driver's education class who had to take the vision portion of the test twice because I couldn't see, and I would have walked a country mile in the snow rather than put my glasses on in class. It wasn't the difficulty of the test. It was my eyes. I had headaches when I would put them on and snatching them off so frequently. There was nothing wrong with my head. It was my eyes. My view of people became more and more distorted. They weren't fuzzy. It was my eyes. I was so glad when they made contacts! My eyesight is still so miserable, I think it made a deal with my ears. If I don't have my contacts in or glasses on (stylish, no more 1080p LED frames), I declare I can't hear! You know it's a done deal when your contacts are multi-focal. Now I can see 20/20 with them since my vision is corrected! Be it middle school or the school of life, things can already be awkward and challenging enough. However, choosing not to correct your vision for fear of what others may think can cause the experience to be more difficult than it already is. Allow purpose to correct your outlook and vision since how you see everything depends on the condition of your eyes.

Your Testament: How do I see myself? How do I view other people? What is my overall outlook on the state of the world? What could distort my vision? How does my vision affect other areas of my life?

Purpose corrects vision and can change your outlook, which is why it is imperative for you to realize your purpose now. Your outlook on life through the eyes of purpose is so much brighter. No, not everything will be rose colored, but you will have a bird's-eye view of peace and have meaning and balance in your life. That insight has a positive rippling effect on your relationships or circle of three to five friends, their circle of three to five and so on. Imagine for a moment if your car manufacturer, home builder, leaders, mechanic, dry cleaner, coworker, most intimate relationship, shoe maker, shop owner, daycare provider, clothier, restaurateur, politician (yes, them, too), barber or beautician, lawyer, accountant, etc. were all involved in their professions because they knew their purpose and carried it out through those missions? What if they had great vision for their lives? Bring it in a little and imagine completely loving who you are and loving what you do, personally and professionally. Imagine having balance and great peace, knowing why you live and what you are doing rather than being self-ignorant and a volunteer for societal puppeteering.

Your Testament: Describe, in detail, what you just imagined. Create questions and answers about that scenario.

_____

_____

_____

_____

_____

_____

What is Purpose?

Your purpose is the alignment of one that affects the continuity of us all. No one has the answers for everything all the time. Your purpose isn't designed to make you some all-seeing solution guru or give the exact answer or a perfect solution for every single issue. However, the answers and solutions that living your purpose grants you will instill consistent peace about the things you know, don't know and never will. Purpose can even make "I don't know" sound smart sometimes. You may never know the answer to world peace or the solution for world hunger, but you can have peace that your purpose is keeping you from being a part of perpetuating the problems. That peaceful assurance makes you aware that accomplishing your mission(s) is a part of numerous interconnected solutions. You consciously have a deliberate effect on the positive results. There are some things you don't know that may be someone else's purpose. Purpose and self-discovery can be compared to the drop in the ocean that affects the entire body of water that it's connected to, the ripple effect. As you continue to discover and execute your purpose, it begins to reveal purpose in what is connected to you; those you influence and those who influence you. There will definitely be strategic and vital connections made with others to thrust and advance your *world of purpose* and theirs. But, don't keep waiting, hoping, or completely relying on anyone else but YOU to make *it* happen!

Again, you don't *have* to realize your purpose for you will innately play your role in the universe, but it is so much more fulfilling and powerful when you compose your part rather than memorize someone else's script, unless acting is your mission. It can mean the difference between being ridden versus driving; you may be traveling, but why, what and how can be a big deal. Not knowing your spiritual identity is like setting out to travel the world without knowing what the world is (lands or seas), what's out there (atmospheres, climates, beauty or danger), how to get there (terrain or transportation) or not knowing where you are, or that going is even a possibility. A journey begins with desire to take it, but you can't enjoy the journey if you are a stranger to the marvelous person who's on it, you! You see, it's not a matter of life or death, but knowing what true life is can determine the quality and satisfy meaning. You can be much more deliberate and confident, and being aware of your experience is the marked difference between simply existing and living.

And, remember your circle of three to five I just mentioned? Think for a moment on how those relationships would be enhanced if all lived their identified purposes and were consistently accomplishing their life's mission with incredible passion. Revel in that thought and feeling for a moment again. Now, imagine again if everyone they know, and at least half of who those people know did the same. The thought of that brings about a sense of peace. Varied forms of abuse, wars, crime, racism, prejudices, and ill intent may only find its place in rarity or possibly non-existent. It's not impossible. Most atrocities are wielded by the hands of those who live in fear, afraid of losing power, money or control. Greed is passion out of control and void of purpose. Those fears can't exist long in the world of purpose for purpose will allow you to see and experience unique wealth and enjoy the peace of consistent provision. Your purpose ensures your access to plenty.

Your Testament: What are my greatest fears? How do I handle fears? What will it mean to overcome them? When am I most brave? What does it mean to me to be fearless?

_____

_____

_____

_____

_____

_____

_____

_____

_____

_____

_____

_____

_____

_____

_____

_____

_____

_____

_____

_____

_____

_____
_____
_____
_____
_____
_____
_____
_____
_____
_____
_____
_____
_____
_____
_____
_____

It's not to be taken to the extreme that purpose creates some Marshmallow World full of fat fairies playing harps, or money and fruit growing on the same tree. But having a life experience where order isn't due to threating governments and the tight-fisted power of power-hungry bullies who live afraid. But, everyone's self-respected path respects and intersects with another's, thereby producing an innate and desired sense of unity and balance. Purpose is only necessary if that is. Is it?

Your Testament: Do I believe knowing my purpose is necessary? Why? Why not?

_____

_____

_____

_____

_____

_____

_____

_____

_____

_____

_____

_____

_____

_____

_____

_____

_____

_____

_____

_____

_____

_____

_____

_____

_____

_____

_____

_____

_____

_____

_____

_____

_____

_____

Once you weigh the necessity, know that your realization of purpose, mission(s) and passion are not one-time experiences. Reading this book from cover to cover ten times over will not do the work of purpose for you. Remember, you need to know this is not simply another self-help book for you to read and close, but, again, your purpose will require you to help yourself or it will frustrate the hell out of you if you don't! Skimming past the questions ignores you and ignoring yourself keeps you ignorant on purpose. Your testimony will be inadmissible if you don't do the work to present the evidence for your life. This is a resource for purpose and an interactive tool for you to do the work of self-discovery. This is an experience! You may want to read some things out loud, especially what you write. You may need to think about what I say, but *do* what YOU say. Commit to living what you read, write and say on purpose.

Your Testament: How am I enjoying self-discovery, thus far? What is the most significant evidence I've discovered, as of yet? What can I begin to implement now?

_____

_____

_____

_____

_____

_____

_____

_____

_____

_____

_____

_____

_____

_____

_____

_____

_____

_____

_____

_____

_____

_____

_____

_____

_____

_____

_____

_____

_____

_____

_____

_____

_____

Reading is essential, but implementation is genius! There must be practical application. Knowing who you are, your spiritual identity will allow you to teach others how to treat you and use purpose as the lesson plan. It will also clarify how you can best relate to them as well. Realizing and knowing your purpose has its privileges and responsibilities. It also has hindrances and benefits. Let's touch on what some of the most common hindrances so they will know you are coming and move! Knowing what some of them are gives you a working knowledge of how deliberately and consistently overcome challenges. Purpose doesn't eliminate all challenges. It deliberately uses them to prove your ability to overcome. It's like the hurdles; they don't stop the race they are part of it, *purposely* put in place to be jumped; overcome and overtaken. Purpose gives your challenges a reason. We'll also establish a few of the unlimited benefits of knowing your spiritual identity so you will know how to remain energized to successfully champion your cause, as you live on purpose and accomplish your missions.

Your Testament: What are some challenges I already know I want to overcome? What can I implement now? What have I discovered about me, thus far?

_____

_____

_____

_____

_____

_____

_____

_____

_____

_____

_____

_____

Chapter Four

POSSIBLE HINDRANCES OF DISCOVERY

⁂

POSSIBLE HINDRANCES OF DISCOVERY

You

What can hinder you from discovering, remembering or realizing who you are? Understanding the hindrances can also reveal the great benefits. The major hindrance in realizing your purpose is you, your own thoughts, beliefs and self-ignorance and self-disobedience. It's not the mouth on your face that you have to contend with, it's the mouth of your mind. Purpose reminds the mouth of your mind that your entire life is listening, with every intent to do! Your mental conversations can be your number one saboteur. What you say to yourself can cause you to be victim of thought bullying. Most prisons aren't bars and buildings, but mental constructs that confine and push you around. It may take repetition and just as much positive effort and planting to roll out and strategically dig up the residuals of negativity in your thoughts. Stop bullying your mind with negative thoughts of self.

Your thoughts are where your ideas, dreams, visions and goals are conceived and should never fear being alone with you.

Thought bullying can be unproductive mental noise or an incessant stream of thoughts bombarding your mind. Or, you can bully your thoughts by allowing negativity to push away or belittle the ones that come to serve your life. That bullying will cause issues with self-esteem and can even induce stress. Self-esteem is what you think about yourself whether your external environment reinforces it or not. Stress is caused by worrying about things that have already occurred or have yet to happen and most things you worry about never happen. It's a mental attempt to override what's happening now. When you are progressive, it's common to have stressful moments, but purpose will keep stress from being a way of life.

Your Testament: How am I being bullied by my thoughts? How are my thoughts being bullied by me? How can I make peace? What are my dreams, visions and goals? What will it mean to achieve them?

_____

_____

_____

_____

_____

_____

_____

_____

_____

_____

_____

_____

_____

_____

_____

_____

_____

_____

_____

_____

Stuck On Repeat?

Most of those folks you think are thinking about you are not, and the ones who may be talking about you; that's usually all they are doing to you. Don't allow your perceived thoughts of what you think they think or have said to be your enemy. Sometimes it's not what people have said, it's what you keep saying to yourself or you may have their words stuck on repeat. People may have told you who they thought you were or were not. Be it during childhood or last night, positive or negative, no matter what happened, it is imperative that you realize: _You are not what happened to you or what you've done—good, bad or indifferent—nor are you just the one who lived through it, but you ARE the one who knew you would!!_ Believe that! Know that!

With that being said, it still doesn't make what you did or didn't do your identifier though it may have been your behavior. Don't allow it to negatively type cast you. Let your purpose-filled lifestyle destroy all the old evidence of ignorance. Own up to what you have done. If you need to do something about it to make it right, handle it! But, don't keep re-living it through mental repetition.

I wonder why people usually put more negativity than positivity on repeat. IF you must repeat, repeat all! I had a client who had been down trodden for over forty years... When she was a little girl one person called her stupid one time. She has since earned a bachelor's degree, master's degree and was working on her doctorate. Do you realize how many times the word stupid felt stupid every time she passed a test, wrote a paper, passed a class, showed up on the Dean's List and graduated with honors from high school and with each degree?! What! Say it ain't so! She had that one millisecond moment stuck on repeat, in full stereo listening with her head... phones. The sound was so real she lived there and her thought-life kept it current and allowed it to bully her. She couldn't hear anything else. She spent years of her life making a very intelligent reality and didn't play that music in her life. If you must play the negative, at least put the positive in, too, and put them on shuffle! At least have balance. I must report she's all tuned up now, playing positivity on repeat and living purpose! One thing that worked for her that you may find helpful is to repeat some things out loud. Especially if the negativity had an external voice, give purpose one out loud, too! The voice of your purpose has the power, privilege and responsibility to be heard. Create a mantra and say it out loud. Strategically placed sticky notes and screen savers are like mini billboards and are great ways to promote positive repetition as well.

Your Testament: What's on the play list of my mind? What are some negative things I've had on repeat? How am I supporting them? What positive affirmations can I repeat to cancel out the negative? How will I support them?

_____

_____

_____

_____

_____

_____

_____

_____

_____

_____

_____

_____

_____

_____

_____

_____

_____

_____

_____

_____

_____

_____

_____

_____

_____

_____

_____

_____

_____

_____

_____

_____

Self-disobedience

You may think it is arrogant to obey yourself. The word *obey* gets a bad rap! It   means to carry out instructions. But, come on, everyone obeys something or someone all the time even when they don't realize it. You obey lines (in the street), lights (traffic), the weather, commercials, sleep, money, the utility company, trash day, a crying baby, clocks, price tags, bad food in the refrigerator, road signs, body odor, an ATM, holidays, etc. If you follow those instructions, why not be obedient to yours? Obeying all of those things promote balance; keep you from harm and even death, as does your spiritual obedience to God in you—*the creative and all sustaining power and connecting life source for all there is*. God is... Don't leave your life completely in the hands of another's decisions or to the inadequate hands of your second-guessing; that wasn't bold enough to come first. It's like the second string on a team; it *may* not be completely horrible, but it can cost you the championship. Second-guessing can cost you more money, time and a lot of frustration with yourself because you know you knew better. Second-guessing can screw up a simple walk in the park.

Your Testament: What lessons have I learned from second-guessing? What has it cost me?

_____

_____

_____

_____

_____

_____

_____

_____

_____

_____

_____

_____

_____

_____

_____

_____

_____

_____

_____

_____

_____

_____

_____

_____

_____

You may be asking, "Who am I to obey myself?" Maybe you've made bad decisions and don't trust yourself enough to carry out your own instructions. Purpose will allow you the courage to trust yourself again. Maybe you didn't know how to listen to yourself or have the awareness to obey. There's no need to identify purpose if you're not going to become what it says. There is no need to look within for instruction if you are not going to be obedient to it. Self-disobedience can cause you to discredit your spiritual intelligence and render yourself unrecognizable. You won't know who you're talking about, much less listening to. Obedience has been so misrepresented and even used to mistreat and abuse. However you recognize authority will directly influence your willingness to obey who you are. Your thought life or the voice of your mind is your greatest influence. How well you listen to yourself and the God in you has a lot to do with how well others listen to you, too. You teach them how to treat you by how you respond to your divinity.

Your Testament: How have I taught others to treat me? Do I enjoy the way I treat myself? What can I change?

_____

_____

_____

_____

_____

_____

_____

_____

_____

_____

_____

_____

_____

_____

_____

_____

_____

_____

_____

_____

_____

_____

_____

Sure, there are situations where you will need to think things through, get advice, confirmation, and develop maturity or partner with others to ensure sensibility and accountability for strategic planning and achievement. That's your self-discovery production team. But, experience self-love by learning to respect your voice and take time to listen, even meditatively. Have you ever thought to do something and when you didn't do it as a result of second guessing or external influence you say, "I *knew* I shouldn't or should have done this or that," or "*Something* told me to do this or that?" It could be as simple as changing lanes while you're driving, taking a different route home, having lunch with a friend, choosing a different product, deciding not to go to an event or just that feeling you get that prompts you to do something outside of your normal routine. It's that pure and simple.

Your Testament: Take a moment to reflect on something recent. Remember how great it felt to have heard and obeyed yourself versus the inconvenience it may have caused not to. Create questions and answers?

_____

_____

_____

_____

_____

_____

_____

_____

_____

_____

_____

_____

_____

_____

_____

_____

_____

_____

_____

_____

_____

_____

_____

_____

_____

_____

A friend of mine was supposed to have been on one of the planes that struck the Twin Towers on September 11, 2001, the day of the terrorists attack. I am grateful that he is still alive today. He listened to himself and changed his travel plans a few days earlier. Self-obedience can be just that serious. On the other hand, on that same unforgettable day, self-disobedience wore me out for five hours! By no means was my situation life threatening, and, looking back on it, it wasn't a big deal. But, the shocking news of the crisis intensified my drama. I was blatantly disobedient. I had discernment, intuition, vibes, tugs, etc., and disobeyed every one of them. I should have spanked myself! My daughter was almost five months old and I had taken her to work with me that morning. Immediately after hearing about what happened in New York, I scooped her up, left work and headed toward home. God, that inner voice that sounds exactly like mine, told me to go buy gas, pampers and some powdered formula for her and get myself some bottled water. But, I let that sorry second-string of thoughts say, "Nah, I have plenty of everything at home and almost a half-tank of gas already." Half-tank *was* a full tank to me. I didn't even buy powdered formula at that time and I wasn't thirsty. Well, I lived on a military base back then and due to the situation, I had no idea they would close the gate to all incoming traffic. She and I sat in bumper-to-bumper traffic for almost five hours, stressed because I could only hear what was going on from the radio and I wanted to see the news on TV! We were hot, and I was thirsty. I kept turning the air conditioner on and off to keep my car, and my baby, from overheating, and to keep from running out of that sorry half-tank of gas, well almost half. I only had one four-ounce bottle of milk and the one she was finishing, one pamper in her diaper bag and one change of clothes. That was all that was in my *be-right-back* diaper bag. I'd left the real one at my parents' house earlier. She was wet, I was thirsty and I felt so helpless! Well you can imagine the rest. It was a doozy! I had both of us crying. I would not have won the Mom of the Year award with that shenanigan. I'll stop telling my story to prevent any of my *bad mom* vibes from gossiping about me again. So, we made it home. She's twelve years old now and doesn't remember a thing! The end.

If I had only listened and obeyed. I had ignored the simple things so many times without consequence that I hadn't developed enough sensitivity to obey me during a crisis moment. I wouldn't have had the feelings of questioning my new mom skills. I created stressful habits that lasted well after the experience. I wouldn't have had issues like carrying an entire baby section that could rival any superstore, in the back of my car, unnecessarily for years. I overbought, overspent and wasted so much time and effort making sure I was always prepared for everything I could think of that pertained to her and probably fourteen other infants and toddlers. . I had socks, onesies, hats, coats, pampers in two sizes, formula and food that eventually expired, toys, stuffed animals, a pop-up playpen, Q-tips, ointment, you name it I had it everywhere all the time. I could have pulled up in any neighborhood or parking lot, popped open the hatch and made some money. Ridiculous! On that frightful day, had I been obedient to my inner voice, it would have only been $25 and a ten-minute trip to the grocery store and about $15 at the gas pump (yes, gas was cheaper then). It could have been even less than that, as I could have traveled five minutes from my job to my parents' house, which was *the* original thought. I heard, but that taught me to listen, be sensitive and obedient to my inner voice. Now, listening to your inner voice doesn't avoid all trouble, issues or challenges, or make you look like Superman, but at least you won't have internal arguments and lose to yourself.

Plus, you won't have to wrestle with guilt. I worked so hard for that disobedience and looked more like Captain Cave Maaan!!!

I used what would be seemingly simple examples to share how something so minor can be a hindrance because if you don't listen and obey that voice when it may not seem to matter that much, it won't be mature or loud enough in situations when it does. What does that have to do with purpose? Everything. If those subtle hints and whispers can't trust you to listen and obey, then the investment decisions, relationship choices, career opportunities, missions, inventions, and creative ideas won't either. Your purpose needs you to be connected and sensitive; listening and obedience are the portals of self-discovery. You can easily hinder yourself and operate unnecessarily out of your natural flow. Self-obedience can save you years of unnecessary disruption, for not only your life, but also everything you affect.

Tradition

You could be reading this book and conclude that if your parents, grandparents, friends and relatives didn't know their purpose, then there's no need for you to know yours either. There is an undercurrent that is very resistant to change, different perceptions, new thoughts and ideas if you allow it. There is a perceived safety when it comes to living inside the box and there is an addictive drug called comfort. So much so, it has its own *zone*. It's all warm and cozy in the box and some people will even fight to remain in a particular pattern of mental behavior even if warm and cozy burns and suffocates. Don't let a box become a coffin. You should enjoy good living and experience life's pleasantries and consistent levels of comfort. But, if you are completely comfortable with everything in your life all of the time, you may be merely existing and not living. Existing versus living is like being on life support or being able to support your life. No biggie?

Change always interrupts comfort and simply living has its share of transition. Transition and evolution are the gradual developments of something dying only to live in another form. That is seen in something as simple yet miraculous as the stages of human development from conception to birth. As warm and cozy as the womb is a baby has got to come out or death is probable, two deaths actually. Once it comes out it is swaddled and held, to be comforted in a different way. Going from comfort to comfort has the discomfort of uncertainty in between. Those who live purposefully are always competing with themselves and exchanging comforts through expressions of betterment—discovering, evolving, creating, implementing and achieving! If your traditions; thinking, believing or doing something the same way as you and yours always have been, and you are very comfortable and *completely* satisfied all the time, STOP READING RIGHT NOW!

Oh, please continue if you must!

Your Testament: What are some of my strongest traditions? How are they affecting my life? What will I have to contend with living with them or without them?

There is something to be said of some traditions, ceremonies and pageantry. They offer a sense of dignity and can demonstrate a level of respect. My dad was a U.S. Marine and my husband is a retired U.S. Navy Corpsman, so he spent his entire career with the Marines. A sailor who was never assigned to a ship, can you believe that? But, a *fine* "doc" he was! So, until 2006, I spent all my life on or around Marine Corps bases. One of the most awesome displays of tradition I've ever witnessed in my life is the Marine Corps Silent Drill Platoon:

Bayoneted rifles flying from Marine to Marine, the lineup of crisp dress blue uniforms, the rhythmic slap of rifles caught by leather-gloved hands: Exemplifying Marine Corps discipline, precision and skill, members of the Silent Drill Platoon are handpicked to represent the Marine Corps. Through intense practice, they learn to perform precise rifle drill movements flawlessly for audiences across America—without a single, verbal command ever spoken. Based at the historic Marine Barracks on 8th and I Streets, SE, Washington, DC, also known as 8th, the Barracks is the oldest, active post in the Marine Corps. Supporting both ceremonial and security missions, the Barracks is the home of the Commandant of the Marine Corps.

They're disciplined and motivational and their presence is amazing. They are not just something to see, but also something to experience. I don't know about any of their screening or training traditions. I would guess some might be treasured secrets that may even strain social acceptance. But, I have seen the evidence of their commitment to training and tradition produce an awe-inspiring performance. The impeccable uniforms, the disciplined, physical frame, the precision of cadence and the stealth orders; they all appear to be close in weight and height, and the way they march is like a rigid swag, as if they ordered *cool* and had it under control. They must have locked Gomer Pyle away in his Quonset hut. It's been years since I've seen them perform live, but no matter how many times I did, I was always so impressed! Can you tell? Not only are they silent, but their quiet authority became contagious to the audience and affects the noise level and movement until there was almost none.

There are traditions within religion, armed forces, sororities, fraternities, clubs and organizations that remind their members of the dignity and respect of the group. Some of our cultures, practices, beliefs and customs have perpetuated a sense of family and belonging, offering a sense of stability and assurance. Some of their benevolence becomes more reaching and powerful from working together rather than be scattered and possibly less effective alone. If that were the case, may the attributes of those traditions continue and may folks continue to join their ranks by leaps and bounds. But, when traditions produce stagnation, prejudice, arrogance or stifles growth or creativity, it can hinder you from recognizing your spiritual identity. They can also create and produce fear. If your traditions impede the process of holistic betterment, it may be time to remove, rework, renovate, or challenge them. If your traditions causes you anguish or you don't even know why you do what you do, it may be time to deny or denounce them. It's difficult to realize your spiritual identity when your human identity is steeped in practices and habits that perpetuate mindless herding. Repeating or doing something only because your mother/father or grandparents did it or said it, those things that are done mindlessly, without cause, reason or justification and produce retardation or negativity can hinder self-discovery.

Your Testament: Traditions: Why do I do it? What does it mean? What is the origin or history behind it? Who started it? How do my traditions add value to my life? You may be surprised at the answers your questions bring back to you. Create your own questions and listen for the answers. Can they trust me to live them or am I sending the questions to fetch the answers in vain?

_____

_____

_____

_____

_____

_____

_____

_____

_____

_____

_____

_____

_____

_____

_____

_____

_____

_____

_____

_____

_____

_____

_____

_____

_____

_____

_____

_____

_____

_____

_____

_____

_____

_____

_____

_____

Especially around holidays and within some families, there are traditions that facilitate dysfunction or the enjoyment of the activity promotes ignorance of the origin. Thanksgiving is an American tradition when we come together to give thanks and enjoy lots of food and spending time with family, but that holiday from American Indian history may offer another perspective. But, it's tradition... One definition of tradition is the passing down of elements of a culture from generation to generation, the way something is usually done, especially by oral communication. Some things that have been deemed as respectable traditions all boil down to someone's unfounded superstitions. The best way to rid yourself of traditions that could hinder your purpose is to ask questions. Don't throw the baby out with the bathwater, some traditions may be harmless or beneficial and if that is the case, enjoy them and carry on. But, some can promote negative repetition and cause generational ruin. It may not even need to be explained. Some of the traditions you may be accustomed to and need to release may already be coming to mind.

Your Testament: What are some of my traditions that I can interview? Write them down and ask them questions as they come, and as many as you can.

_____

_____

_____

_____

_____

_____

_____

_____

_____

_____

_____

_____

It could be that it may not be the origination or foundation of the tradition, but an archaic, warped or diluted interpretation that interrupted the original intent. Some traditions try to time themselves out and you don't want to let them go, out of habit, especially if you feel it is letting someone go. You may not have to change the tradition, but rather the way you think about it. Allow your deliberate questioning, time and purpose to naturally evolve it, interpret, implement and consistently practice it. You have to decide if your traditions are effective.

Your Testament: Do my traditions serve me now or am I enslaved by them? What traditions need to be updated or upgraded? Am I proud of my traditions? Are my traditions proud of me? How can I require my traditions to evolve?

_____

_____

_____

_____

_____

_____

_____

_____

_____

_____

_____

_____

_____

_____

_____

_____

_____

_____

_____

_____

_____

_____

_____

It may feel awkward or cause a real sense of vulnerability, but the freedom of knowing your spiritual identity will continually fill the *temporary* void. You may have to clean out some things in order to receive. If you struggle with trying to find new ways to do the same, old thing different, it may be high time to create a whole new something else to do. By now, an old ill-fitting tradition may be tired of you, too, like a cheap pair of dress shoes, and you can appreciate one another for the relief of release by stepping out! So don't fret, your purpose and creativity are well equipped and ready to discover and sustain a brand new *do* for you. The traditions you decide to maintain can support your purpose and those you release will let you go, too. Either they will embrace you or they may push you out.

Your Testament: What are some new traditions I can create that support my life and my discovery? How will I implement them? When will I start?

_____

_____

_____

_____

_____

_____

_____

_____

_____

_____

_____

_____

_____

_____

_____

_____

_____

_____

_____

_____

_____

_____

_____

_____

_____

Beliefs

Just like traditions, some of your beliefs may be tired of you, too. A belief is a mental habit that usually has behavioral evidence. It may not be that certain beliefs are a direct hindrance that could keep you from knowing your purpose, but how much you believe them can reveal how you will believe your purpose. An authentic belief has phases. You hear or see something, and you think about it, understand it, test it, believe it, know it and live it. Some of your beliefs may be stuck at a phase between hearing and testing, and you are only acting as if you're living it—that's *make believe* and hypocrisy's biggest promoter. A weak belief system can hinder your purpose because not only are you supposed to believe your beliefs, but your beliefs believe you, too.

Your Testament: What do I believe about myself? How can my purpose use those beliefs? Why do I believe them? What beliefs believe me?

_____

_____

_____

_____

_____

_____

_____

_____

_____

_____

_____

_____

_____

_____

_____

_____

_____

_____

_____

_____

_____

_____

Instability in your current belief system will bring that same mental behavior into the realization of your purpose and implementation of who you are. Whatever attributes of Deity you are depending on are depending on you, too. Living your purpose requires a solid commitment to who you are. You have to believe in you, who you say you are and what you are doing and believe you have the ability to do it. You may need reinforcements, but they will take cues from you. If you approached your beliefs now with uncertainty, as if they are swaying opinions, how do you expect new ones to come to you and develop wholeheartedly? Your beliefs are your mental acceptance about the truth of something, including you. Your beliefs may be based on upbringing, traditions, religion, creeds, cultures, and their varied interpretations. Take inventory of what you believe and try not to be afraid to ask and answer. Also, be aware of the beliefs you no longer believe, yet try to convince others to believe. Something as seemingly innocent as Santa Claus, the Tooth Fairy, the Boogie Man and the Easter Bunny are traditions, but they are based on a strong societal belief system that the innocence of children is preserved by deception. Regardless of the historical record of such holiday icons, most adults do not believe in the characters, but will strategically sell the idea to children and we literally buy into it all the way. The retailers believe you will and you probably don't let them down. It is not for me to question your beliefs; your purpose has assigned that job to you. Just do so with vigor because a belief that cannot be questioned and answered is probably an opinion that's too weak to live or a fantasy that has gone rogue.

People create these mental habits and believe they are supposed to pass them on to children. It really doesn't matter how warm and fuzzy it makes you feel, these beliefs aren't true. I celebrate Christmas and other holidays, but my husband and I didn't choose to tell our daughter to believe in Santa Claus. Nor did we weigh down the innocence of her youth with reality to set her up to have to confront adults and her peers. The adults are worse than the kids are! It doesn't seem like a big deal until your child tells another child the truth when the adults in their lives are working hard to keep up the lie. Oh boy! It can mess up a neighborhood! Some lies are so big the truth looks mean, so folks just go with it. But, we told her the truth, tenderly, and used wisdom to answer her questions. I couldn't see trying to get her to believe that a strange man in a red suit would come to our home, while we were asleep, to drop free toys down a chimney we didn't have. Nor could we see not giving her an opportunity to imagine. When she began to ask those strong questions, the belief couldn't carry the weight and we would have had to tell lies on top of lies to perpetuate a weak belief. Don't allow a weak belief to use your creativity. You create a lie in order to make them believe more lies about the first one. It cut out the drama of creating deception, so in her world Santa Claus wasn't something to believe in he was a fairy tale, like Mickey Mouse. She could have the fantasy and use her imagination and we could help her enjoy it, but the key is belief.

Blame

As an adult, you really can't justifiably blame someone else for your life or your beliefs because, as long as you live, beliefs always have access to new information. You just can't keep blaming yourself for what you didn't know or what no one taught you to be in your personal life, relationships or in business/career. But, you can decide to be responsible for what you're willing to believe and learn now. Don't volunteer to be a victim of the *pride bully* by not asking someone to help you achieve and do well in YOUR school of life. In some instances, you may be quick to blame which is another possible hindrance of recognizing your purpose.

Sometimes you may have to forgive yourself and sometimes you will have to forgive others. Whoever the people were in your life that may not have been positive they are no longer there now. If they are, purpose will allow wisdom to teach you the tool of riddance. Sometimes it's not the riddance of the people/person, but riddance of the residue of dysfunction, the blame. It may seem harsh, but whatever was done happened then. Blaming someone else now for your current situation gives them power over your life. If there was criminal activity get legal assistance, if psychological issues stemmed from the situation, seek professional, mental help. Holding on won't change the story and passing the blame does not change the deed. But, when you blame someone, you render yourself powerless to change and grow. Wherever the blame rests, so does the power. It is not to be implied that you should just move on when there are deep issues yet to confront. As I said, in certain cases, you may need to seek specific forms of therapy, counseling, professional life coaching or even the attention of the authorities. No one is expecting you to *just get over it*, but you have to decide to only allow the facts of past negativity to tell your story if it has the courage to show up positive.

For instance, my family experienced its share of dysfunction, struggle as well as laughter, achievement and success, which I, at one time, really felt left out. I felt different early on, which makes me so comfortable with being somewhat different now. It was because of an innocent childhood prank gone long. My siblings played a joke on me when I was around five years old by showing me a fictitious adoption certificate and telling me I had been adopted. How creative was that?! I couldn't read and had no reason to doubt. Initially, I don't even think I really knew what it meant. Some very minor differences in how we were treated reinforced my belief over the years. The differences in treatment were, since they were older they had later bed times, more freedoms and during those *rare* times we were given money, they got a little more. My sister got to wear her hair out, but I had to wear plaits and ponytails. I had to stay on our street when I rode my bike, my brother could go all over the neighborhood. They got to stay after school and play sports but I was a latchkey kid. I didn't do the math at that age to realize it was due to the fact they were four and five years older than I am. I thought it was because I was adopted.

The innocent prank ended with them the same day it was played, but it lived on secretly within me until I was almost fourteen years old. I never asked. I didn't tell. I believed I was adopted until I saw my birth certificate for the first time when I was in the eighth grade; I had to take it to school. Talk about drama that day! My siblings forgot all about it, but I lived nine years of my life thinking I was adopted. Immediately one may capitalize on the negatives that something of that nature can justify blame. But, what would blaming do (WWBD)? How would blaming have helped my life? What would it change? What would it do? To blame good kids for an old prank wouldn't change a thing. Plus it would render me powerless to use the situation for my good. My sister and brother did not know I would be deceived for years. They didn't know my belief would last longer than their intention. I couldn't blame myself either; I didn't know any better. I was only five, cute, too.

Funny thing was that it wasn't the certificate alone or them telling me I was adopted, but there were also relatives in Portsmouth, Virginia, where I was born, who didn't know my mom and dad had me before we moved to MCAS Cherry Point, North Carolina. So the idea of adoption was reinforced at every family gathering and relatives would say to my parents, "Where did she come from? Oh, I didn't know you had another one! When did you have this one?" I thought, *How jacked (rude)! Did they have to ask right in front of me? Dang!* But, then again, I felt strong and I felt like because I secretly knew already, they were the ones who had to feel uneasy.

When I became aware of my own purpose and life's mission I would see where thinking I was adopted was an incredible preservative. Instead of blame, which would have been a hindrance for realizing who I am, at a young age I used that to separate myself from typical peer pressure and negative adolescent behavior. My siblings got a little rowdy; typical during teenage years and, my thinking we weren't really related caused me to not follow suit, deliberately. But, thankfully, it also caused me to appreciate my family so much because the '70s and '80s were rough around my way and I thought it was so kind of them to love me, want me and take me in. Isn't that something? It also made me feel comfortable with thinking and being different…still. It made me solid about my uniqueness and individuality and established a thought process that makes me so accepting of others to this day. So, blame who for what? If nothing else, I appreciate the affect and I love my sister and brother. Everything happens for a reason and you have to allow the seemingly good and bad to run parallel to promote balance.

My story may not be the worst of the worst or the best of the best, but it is an example how to stop passing blame. Now you may have had a situation that it is in your best interest and theirs to leave some folks alone. Not passing blame doesn't mean you are friends. Not passing blame may just mean they stay where they are and you do the same. Not passing blame doesn't mean you call somebody and rehash some dusty drama. Not passing blame may just be having the freedom to let it go so *it* can let you go, too. You have to decide when to forgive, and how to forgive, but you must forgive! All that's been said about blame could have also been said about forgiveness, but I've seen people who forgive and still use the situation as a point of reference to perpetuate the negative effects. Saying, "I forgave him, but if he hadn't done that I would be better off now!" or "I had to forgive myself for doing that, but that's why I still don't like any of them anymore to this day!" They forgive the deed, but to keep passing blame creates excuses for current issues. Forgiving is for you and choosing not to continue to blame is for them. Let go! Blaming bears no fruit, not even blaming you! Empower yourself by removing the weight of blame and know that who you are right now may or may not be the best you've ever been, but it's not the best you will ever be! Don't allow blaming others to hinder you and attempt to strip you of your God-given power to discover and achieve. No matter what *they* said or did, say or do how you choose to handle your life is beyond their control! No blame. Don't keep answering the call of negativity by mentally resuscitating it. Don't give negativity the pleasure, power or responsibility of being an influential presence throughout the stages of your life.

Your Testament: What am I blaming someone else for? What am I blaming myself for? What are some areas I may need help in? What am I willing to learn?

_____

_____

_____

_____

_____

_____

_____

_____

_____

_____

_____

_____

_____

_____

_____

_____

_____

_____

_____

_____

_____

_____

Procrastination

Procrastination is putting things off out of laziness, carelessness, disrespect and habitually putting things off, results in putting you off, which can hinder the discovery and implementation of purpose. Until when? Sometimes the most lame excuses or *until-itis* can nudge folks full of potential inch-by-inch, right into the grave. *Until-itis* is one of procrastination's best tools and can weaken progress and achievement. It occurs when you think or say things like wait *until* I get some money, *until* it warms up/cools off, *until* I get married/divorced, *until* I get a promotion/retire or *until* they do/don't do this or that. *Until-itis* has a way of causing dis-ease in other areas until what you could do doesn't want you anymore. *Until-itis* may have allowed you to become expired to the highest realm of betterment! But, don't worry purpose allows you to reset or create anew, which can happen through the art of transition's wake up call. It has a funny way of curing *until-itis*. But, why wait to be pushed?

Your Testament: What are some things I have been waiting *until* to do? Why? What can I begin to implement now? How can I be accountable? How can I be consistent?

_____

_____

_____

_____

_____

_____

_____

_____

_____

_____

_____

_____

_____

_____

_____

_____

_____

_____

_____

_____

_____

_____

_____

Procrastination has a way of distorting perception, allows you to play stupid with purpose, sleep on your dreams and enlists you to be the number one enemy of your goals. The crazy thing about it is, once you accomplish something you've been putting off, you usually wonder why you didn't do it sooner and self-ignorance is the culprit. Most of the things you procrastinate about have more to do with the things that affect you more so than things that affect other people in your life. You show up for their wants and go AWOL on your needs. Folks talk about deadbeat parents who won't supply a fundamental need for their children in some way, so don't behave deadbeat toward you! Show up, show up on time, and take advantage of the custody you have of your life and don't miss or skip out on those precious visitations with time. Procrastination also breeds frustration and stress because your mind knows you are out of sync with what you know you are supposed to be doing. The best time to annihilate self-ignorance and live on purpose is now. Procrastination can have your mind on what you should be doing and missing the gift of the present moment. Time is on your side and procrastination steals or abuses it. Treat time like a friend, respect it and it won't run out on you. Use it as one of the tools of your mission. It's not against you.

Your Testament: What am I procrastinating about? What satisfaction am I getting by not doing it? What will it take for me to do it? When?

_____

_____

_____

_____

_____

_____

_____

_____

_____

_____

_____

_____

_____

_____

_____

_____

_____

_____

_____

_____

_____

_____

_____

_____

_____

_____

_____

_____

_____

_____

_____

Entertainment

The most common hindrance to discovering your purpose can be entertainment. Entertainment may be *the* culprit for so much procrastination, useless traditions, warped beliefs and unproductive blame. You may be thinking that being entertained is harmless and is a way to relax your mind. It is! In healthy doses, entertainment can allow your mind and thought processes a much needed break and even spark new thoughts, incite creativity, and broaden awareness. The key is *healthy* doses. Some people need a break from entertainment instead of using entertainment as a break. A synonym for the word entertainment is the word distraction as well the word pleasure. Entertainment is an *act* (yes, act!) that is diverting and holds the attention using amusement. But, even those who are paid to entertain us work to get our attention. They put in time to create and are disciplined and skilled in their craft to make us believe. We make watching people act a big part of our reality. That is amusing, isn't it? Amusement is the activity that diverts thoughts or puts a pause in between times of focus. Entertainment is meant to be a noticeable break, shifting your reality to provide pleasure and a way to pass time. It's an enjoyable pause, not a marathon of negligence. Go to work and spend your whole day at lunch or in the break room if you want to and see what happens. Amusement as a way of life is for clowns. Could that be where your time is going or the how you may have contracted *until-itis*?

Your Testament: What is diverting my attention? What has my attention? Why? How long is it being held? What is happening in my life that would cause me to feel I need to be distracted and pass this much time?

_____
_____
_____
_____
_____
_____
_____
_____
_____
_____
_____
_____
_____
_____
_____
_____
_____
_____
_____
_____
_____

Ask yourself and decide to have the courage to accept the answers that come to you. You could take time right now to ask and listen to your answers and choose to become or do what they say. Please do! Implementation is crucial!

Too much mindless entertainment could be the reason why in a world of microwaves, cars, flights and fast money you feel you still don't have enough time in a day. And of course, we have fast food. Forefathers used to have to plant it, tend it, harvest it, walk, wait, carry, clean it and cook it before they ate it. We get anxious at the drive-thru. We have grocery stores, digital, virtual and one touch! Be it print or social media, sports, computers, gaming or TV, it's up to you not to use entertainment to sabotage purpose and self-discovery.

Sure you can enjoy wonderful times of entertainment to relax and be pleasured by doing nothing, including watching TV or gaming, but schedule them, record them, make them serve your purpose—so your entertainment habits won't destroy the gift of time, while you watch and listen to an act! You may even be critical of their acting while you hypocritically miss out on your truth. It's something how TV allows you to watch the lives of others (fiction, sports, reality, news, etc.) and you haven't held yourself as accountable to watch your own. If watching someone else's extremely dysfunctional reality is entertaining, what in the world is happening in the real lives of the viewers? Maybe the sensations of seeing craziness elsewhere temporarily relieves the pain of personal situations or makes folks feel better about their own drama. Your purpose is not going to be discovered or advanced if your entertainment is not disciplined. Entertainment will go rogue on your intentions if allowed. TV, gaming or any activity that simultaneously bombards your senses (seeing & hearing) can divert you for such long periods of time that your reality becomes dysfunctional, goes undefined or outright sucks. I guess that could be life imitating art and vice versa. You can experience positive things from entertainment or even be inspired.

Your Testament: How is entertainment affecting my productivity? How can I use it positively?

_____

_____

_____

_____

_____

_____

_____

_____

_____

_____

_____

_____

_____

_____

_____

_____

_____

_____

_____

_____

_____

_____

_____

_____

This book could be a form of entertainment if you're only reading it for the sake of information and not implementation. If you are creating your testament, implementing and doing your work, it *is* work. So TV and other forms of media aren't altogether bad either. They only become a hindrance to purpose if your times of pleasured distraction and diversion (entertainment) have more influence on your life than the reality of your purpose. Maybe you can upgrade your entertainment to a creative activity like writing your testament, reading and applying helpful material, painting, learning to play an instrument, a new language, singing, playing a sport, dancing, etc. or picking up an activity you used to enjoy. That way when entertainment is called for, you have multiple options. You can actively enjoy your reality and not being held hostage to the QWERTY keyboard, game controller, enslaved to the couch and solely by the creativity of someone else.

Your Testament: How does entertainment affect my life? How can I upgrade my entertainment? What can I upgrade it to?

_____

_____

_____

_____

_____

_____

_____

_____

_____

_____

_____

_____

_____

_____

_____

_____

_____

_____

_____

_____

_____

_____

_____

Entertainment also includes the marketing of retail and the repetition can be an all-out assault on your mind instead of it becoming relaxed and pleasured. You have multiple senses being bombarded at the same time. You know that's how a grocery store sampling booth works. You see it, hear about it and smell it at the same time and the next thing you know, your mouth is feeling, your tongue is tasting and you just used a coupon and paid somebody to take it home to do to it all again, all caused by the effects of a sample on your senses. Some commercials are like a top ten count down. They repeat incessantly and without effort you can quote it, sing it, talk about it and then before you realize you're buying things your purpose doesn't even require and then when your purpose does require something, your money has already taken the other job. Imagine if you were that way with positive affirmations and actions... But, it feels good to buy and enjoy the things you like because you genuinely like them not because you were conditioned to. Enjoy that. And when you get those things you like, make sure you are using them to be reflective of who you are and not being used by them to expose self-ignorance.

Commercialism and stardom are entertaining influences, you see it and you want it exactly like that. Be it a car, hair, clothes, money, vacation, mate, personality, body, muscles, status, Hollywood ideals, etc. And when your attempt doesn't measure up to what has entertained you, your purpose may appear unfulfilling before it has even had the chance to emerge. Maybe you think entertainment isn't a hindrance for you or ineffective. Find out. Turn the TV, game, PC or laptop off for five minutes to an hour, during your normal, peak times of use. Close the magazine, sign out and log off. Be still and see if the silence feels uncomfortable. Old folks used to say, "An idle mind is the devil's workshop." Well,

I believe the worst tinkering is done in a mind that is too busy. I don't want a mind that can't mind me. Silence isn't idle any way; it's like the Silent Drill Team, proving the ability of authority and the control of your life without other voices saying a word! Do you have it or not? Try it! Find out and see how good you've got it. Once you get beyond the awkwardness of the silence, watch how your mind immediately kicks into gear about something you can be thinking or doing that is usually more productive and purposeful. Set some order by calling a quiet cadence, even if it's getting much needed rest. If those aren't your vices, try it with that cell phone that's glued to your hand. Trust me. It *can* be turned off.

Your Testament: How long was I able to go without my regular entertainment? What was that experience like? What thoughts did I have? How was it beneficial? How can I create a plan or schedule to enjoy entertainment instead of being conditioned or ordered by it?

_____

_____

_____

_____

_____

_____

_____

_____

_____

If silence is nerve-racking or too loud, try turning on some relaxing, instrumental music until it becomes more palatable. Whatever you prefer—gaming, your smartphone, laptop, Internet, sports, etc.—entertainment or being entertained alone is only a hindrance if you allow it to be. So, let's not go to a cultish extreme. Just realize that too much is desensitizing and irresponsible. It may be imperative that you shut down the distraction, so you can open up to your purpose. Use entertainment as a profitable tool not a sabotaging habit.

Chapter Five

WHAT IS YOUR PURPOSE?

WHAT IS YOUR PURPOSE?

Your Purpose

Purpose is waiting on you to realize who you are so the things that need you to do them can know and identify you, too. Now that you are more aware of possible hindrances of purpose, what is Your Purpose? When asked, "Who are you?" You may answer that question by stating your name. But, your name is a social identifier and a link for heritage. Your occupation may be an aspect of your mission or how you've chosen to use acquired skills to earn an income. Your titles are probably ordinary explanations of your duties. So now, who are you? That *shower you*—the only one. How do you express that reason? What is your level of passion? Do you know? Does anyone else know? It's so easy to use occupations, education and relationship status or even the most popular social and professional affiliations to reply. That's great data for the Census Bureau, an employment or social application or even a well-scripted bio for any type of candidacy. It's factual information, but your name just boils down to an arrangement of consonants and vowels or associations that make up your social identifier. In most cases, someone else has at least one of those same names, too. The name people call you is *not* you! Your occupation describes what you do, your educational and professional statuses describe what you've accomplished now and your relationship status reveals your family ties and associations. These are things about you, not you.

The Atlantic Ocean is the name of one of the many bodies of water. The letters A-t-l-a-n-t-i-c O-c-e-a-n is what the body of water is called, but it is not the water itself. The letters aren't wet, house no sea life and contain no salt. In no way could those thirteen letters be that ocean. I spent most of my life living near the Atlantic Ocean and I loved going to the beach, especially at night. It is majestic, enchanting, comforting, soothing, and romantic and provided the perfect environment to clear and organize my thoughts, meditate, and write. The letters in the name is what I called it, but to think a name alone would ever do that for me. To think consonants and vowels could ever *be* the sound of waves, smell of the salt, the crisp affect it has on the air and the awesomeness of depth is absolutely ridiculous! The ocean is a life-sustaining, food-bearing, perfect habitat for plant life and fish; it is biological power, no matter where it flows, and is part of a continuous body of water that covers over 70% of the Earth, containing around 97% of the Earth's water supply. It's so much more than a name, huh?

Like the ocean, your name is just a name, your job is what you do, and your accomplishments and affiliations simply reveal your ability to perform and maintain connections. That's good! It may be frightening to some not to depend on names, titles and status to convey who you really are. It may be perceived like a stripping away of all that you are. Who are you? You are beyond names and titles that support your purpose. However, who you are, the *shower you*, is a spiritual powerhouse containing a representation of the attributes that connect to your finite humanity to the infiniteness of God. Once you know your purpose and begin to live it consistently, you immediately have the privilege and responsibility to ask and know the purpose of everything around you. Just be ready for the answers or the lack thereof.

From One Purpose to Another

To assist you with your discovery I felt it would be interesting and helpful for me to share some initial highlights of mine. I know my life matters and as I began to execute the matters of my life, I realized how awesome it is, you, too! I wished I would have known how to ask for help. But, my not knowing or not being able to overcome the fear of asking for help is profitable for you; I have gladly become what I needed. Help can come in the form of agents, counselors, certified life coaches, clergy, mentors, teachers, assistants, and advisors. My culture and upbringing didn't permit me to get *help*. If I had asked for help beyond the church and school it would be concluded that I was not *living right*, was being disobedient or a little crazy for real. I was limited to my block or, should I say, my box. So I went deeper into my box and began to ask questions until dissatisfaction made the lid slip off all by itself because the unanswered questions made my box overflow. I wasn't angry, but frustrated. I didn't mention friends and family as a source for help and some can be. But, because you love them dearly and vice versa those relationships can sometimes be the most difficult to discover and change in. They love and like you the way you are, your life has become convenient in theirs and an interruption may not be well received. I've helped many people discover who they are and, based on our experiences, there have only been rare successful occurrences where the initial team consisted of those most familiar. But, if you feel your friends and family may be your best route, take them.

Your Testament: Who is on my self-discovery production team?

_____

_____

_____

_____

_____

_____

_____

_____

_____

_____

I had gotten to a place in my life where I was happy with the outside relationships and activities in my life, but something inside me just wasn't satisfied with me. I chose to take some time to ask my *shower self* the questions busyness conditioned me to avoid, and I was always watching the plane I wanted to be on taxi down the runway and I missed it, too scared to travel. I wasn't achieving anything that mattered to me. That's how the lid to my box started slipping off...

All this talk about spirituality, purpose, awakening, consciousness, destiny, self-discovery, vision, etc. started with me in 1989/90 and it was blowing my mind, but dead to my life. When it was all said and done, I experienced a spiritually charged setting or a life-changing conversation, the questions of my reality still remained, so...what does all this stuff have to do with who I am? Why am I here? What does all of that have to do with who is going to wash the dishes?! There was no connection for practical application, no me testament, and there was a huge divide for implementation. I was blessed with such rich biblical teaching. I wasn't preached at, I was taught and I thank my parents for that. I got to a point where I had intake overload on biblical, spiritual and self-help information, but I could not translate that or implement it into my reality of how to help myself satisfactorily. I heard people say, "Get out of the box," but I didn't know I was in one, nor how I got in it. I thought, *If were to step out, where do I plant my foot? What is outside the box and if the box was so bad how come so many people were in one?* Then my box escape was drawing me to a culture where I didn't seem to fit in either. I liked nice things, I wanted financial freedom, I wanted to experience a unique variety of healthy fame, I liked comfort, I wanted to create a legacy of wealth and financial comfort and I wanted to matter, be relevant.

My perception of what I was embarking upon, challenged my beliefs, not to change them, but sometimes we only believe what we believe is because that's all we know how to believe. My questions were getting my answers from an unlimited spirituality I wasn't sure my beliefs were mature enough to embrace. Even the language; words like consciousness, purpose and awareness seem to flow with the lifestyle of a Tibetan Monk, or someone who was skipping around and flighty, wearing flowers and ribbons while playing finger cymbals, or having to live directly under the moon— among the wild animals, be homeless, shoeless, and live on a diet of berries and wild pheasants. Me?! Be a monk? I'm a woman, I liked sex, was very happily married, I liked living in a house, I wasn't going to part with my shoes, I had too much sense to be flighty, never really cared to wear ribbons, wasn't a flower kind of girl, the finger cymbals were kind of sexy though, but berries wouldn't do. I wouldn't want any wild animals over as company and what in the hell was I supposed to do with a pheasant, especially a wild one? It's funny now, but I became frustrated with having an internal awareness I could not figure out how to apply to my own life especially when it conflicted with my some of my religious traditions.

I began to realize that no one I knew could help me with my initial decision to change me or take on the responsibility for me to grow into the purpose of my life. If it meant I had to be the answer I wanted to see and become a trailblazer and leader, I would have to do the work of purpose and the toughest thing was realizing that my beliefs and my life had to sync. Because any distance between purposeful answers and practical application leaves too much room for insanity. I had to get it together. It would take some time and it would take work. The work of purpose. But, I was so ready!

I needed help with my life and I was ashamed to say, plus I didn't know who to ask.

When I did venture to ask I was plagued with the skepticism of being thought of as a troublemaker or crazy, be rejected or becoming a slave to someone who would use my questions to create an agenda of their own. I didn't fear being different, I already had that on lock, but I did fear this difference being way too much, like showing off an extra big toe or a third eye. I was used to being an acceptable *different*, but that toe was trying to get out and that eye was trying to see everything!

I couldn't figure out how to ease this process out. The more free I felt on the inside, the more I felt external resistance. I was free internally, but I was being *promoted* to becoming more of a part of a system and lifestyle of creating box instructions for everyone else. I knew there was excellence in a level of uniformity, but I just didn't feel the uniforms all had to be the same size, as long as each of us committed to use our unique abilities, live our purpose and do our best. Understand? I found out then you have to be sensitive if you decide to ask someone about your purpose to ensure their agenda isn't to bind you to theirs and so you aren't giving them your responsibility to discover yours. But, don't be afraid, you live, you learn and so will they. But, I didn't ask mainly because most of the people I knew asked me questions and based on most of their questions, I knew my solutions didn't stand a chance to come to me from their school of thought. And when I did venture to ask, I was told things I think folks only wanted me to hear or I was given, general encouragement that could work from a birthing room to a funeral. You know that *everything will be fine and keep doing good*. I mean, it's true, but that's true for everybody all of the time! I was like, nope, what is *everything*? And please define *good* because I don't know why I'm doing some of the things I am doing and I don't want to do them anymore! Is that good? Or they'd give me a scripture that didn't match my need. It wasn't gospel to me; the good news; the solutions I longed to know, even if they were going to be hard. Daniel in the lion's den didn't have a John Brown thing to do my particular issue at hand, not even a Stretch Armstrong stretch. I wasn't angry with anyone or my religious beliefs…still! But, at least they tried… I'm so grateful for that! I appreciate the sense of community, relationship building and fellowship in a spiritual setting that going to a balanced, local church can offer. I'm grateful for discovering my gifts of administration, singing and songwriting among my AFC church family back then. Some of my most prized relationships are with those I've met in that environment, and still happily reminisce about the times we laughed ourselves to tears, laughing with and at one another when we'd get together. That was great and I knew I was frustrated with my own imbalance and tired of achieving what I thought everyone thought I was supposed to. I was tired of my cycle, the clichés and lingo that lost its vigor and didn't translate where I knew purpose wanted to take me. Based on my religious experience there were some things that going to church, teaching, listening, taking notes, singing, praying, fasting, going to the altar, being told I was free just to reveal flaws that killed the freedom, revivals and conferences, did not meet my desire for more and I didn't even know what *more* was. I was satisfied with pouring into them, but I wasn't filling me. Remember, these are my experiences...

So, I moved geographically, spiritually and mentally. I had to go within, still my mind, step away, walk away, listen and check in with my *shower self* through my three credit reporting agencies (spirit, soul and body.) It took time, prayer, mediation, asking the hard questions and sometimes not getting the answers I wanted to hear, yet getting rejected in every way, but enjoying the power of accepting myself, confronting confusing beliefs that couldn't stand the test and being strengthened by cultivating the ones that would change my life.

When I first tried to meditate, it was like the Macy's Thanksgiving Day Parade and the Bud Billiken parade going on at the same time. By the time I'd sit down, ten things would come to mind that I *should* be doing. Initially, I gave into them; they got me. I'd get a quiet ten seconds tops, not due to others interrupting, but my doggone parade of me interrupting myself! The moment I sat down, I'd pop right up to do something I thought I'd forgotten to do. Eventually, I had to allow it all to come and pass right on by—bands, floats and all.

All I could do was smile and wave. I prayed and I cried sometimes, too. Grocery lists, laundry, phone calls, work, guilt, sins, family issues, plans, fantasies, positive ideas, negative imaginations, etc., I would take a few minutes and not resist them. The less I resisted, the less they persisted. I knew how to pray, but when it came to meditation, I learned that it wasn't something I had to do, per se, but the stillness I had to allow. It took some time, but I was able to enjoy the pleasure of rejuvenation through mental relaxation. I met myself and no longer feared my truths like strangers.

I wrote a lot! A little of what you're reading now surfaced after times of sacred silence. I also realized I didn't have to pray and meditate long. After all, I had my family and me, I still had work, school, church, other people, at one point the transition of living in a foreign country and all the other responsibilities of mission productivity. But, I was more in touch with what my purpose was producing in me. I decided to do the hard thing. Trust the answers I received, and live them anyway. It wasn't as difficult as I thought; my mind had inflated the negative and ignored the peace.

It was hard at first—to appreciate and respect personal solutions and not look for religious, societal, cultural or familiar validation—as my achievements were tied up in *they*. I didn't realize that *they* weren't asking as much of me as I thought they were. I had given my imagination to people's thoughts and perceptions that they didn't even have time to have of me. Those who may have had negative thoughts kept it or got caught up in fruitless deeds. God allowed my thoughts, my answers and the implementation to achieve. I began to do the work and allowed the God in me to become what I needed. I realized I was enough. Initially, it seemed so cocky and selfish, but I had to find out my purpose in order to know the part of God I am. I had to build a purposeful relationship with me in order to have one with you. Internal work and achievement makes my reality, and the external achievement feel like a journey that has already taken place. I am supposed to be here because the God in me purposed it that way. If achievements were solely based on the external, a cutthroat, stressful, toxic rat race would be initiated every five minutes. Oh! Could that be what's going on in the world?

Labels

Is that what was going on with me? I had to deal with my own ideas of achievement and labels. Sometimes we get caught up in labels. We get layered in labels until who we really are gets buried under all of that and the *shower you* seems weak and puny. I have never been one to be too caught up in designer or brand name labels, but I was controlled by the labels I thought people thought I should be. But, purpose gave me permission to put my brand on labels instead of having the labels brand me! I had to remove the mental and some of the imposed functions that were stifling the awareness of my purpose. Sometimes people will give you a label suitable for their destinations and sometimes that's okay as long as you don't miss yours.

You may be good at your labels, but are you able to be guided by authenticity or are you a label parasite being controlled by external cues? The labels are in your hands to decorate your life not hold it together. The divine person you are here to be has the wisdom to decide if the titles and functions are worthy of your identity. You make them look good and they serve you, they are not your masters. Those things are only negative if they hinder you from being able to identify who you truly are or breed suppression that keeps others from discovering theirs. The core of you, your spirit and soul, who knows, sees and hears you like no one else can. The wisdom of purpose will let you know whether to accept the label for your use or keep your hands in your pocket so you aren't misused. No worries your purpose is always here; always has been, alive and well. It most definitely needs you to know it so it can be empowered through implementation and practical application.

Don't get me wrong we all have labels. I'm a black woman who is a mother, wife, daughter, sister, friend, business owner, life coach, teacher, author, speaker, I was raised Christian, I've been a federal, state and local government employee, etc., but those things are function labels. They are what I do or what I did, but in no way, shape or form are they the sum total of who I am without all of that, the God in me is. The *shower me* is. Many people have the same labels, so the labels can't be the sum total of who they are, you or me either. We exist beyond them! If we weren't those titles and some of those labels, we would still be! Labels decorate and accent the *house of my life*, but they are not my foundation, infrastructure. They categorize, describe how I function and tell you about me, they are not me, or you.

Your Testament: What labels am I wearing? How well do they suit me? What labels would I like to get rid of? Why?

_____

_____

_____

_____

_____

_____

_____

_____

_____

_____

_____

My spiritual identity; my purpose, is wisdom, peace, integrity, abundance, laughter and success—all being revealed during different stages of my life and some years apart. The opposite of my identity met me along the way, too. My mission(s); all of which consistently involved me helping myself and others discover solutions, appreciate their uniqueness and encouraging them live better lives, has been though being a daughter, sister, friend, wife, mother, graduate, accounting tech, secretary, administrator, member, songwriter/lyricist, singer, producer, leader, executive secretary and the list goes on. All of those titles and missions allowed my purpose to be visible and in some cases tangible. My passion, level of intensity changes especially when I segue from one mission to another, or when I need to refresh or create, but remains constant to serve who I am and why I do what I do. But, no matter who I am with or what I do wisdom, peace, integrity, abundance, laughter and success are present. I continue to journey in self-discovery, they intensify and may even draw out more attributes of my spiritual identity.

Chapter Six

IT'S YOUR TURN!

IT'S YOUR TURN!

On Your Mark

This is it!! You will never be more you than you already are. But, you can always discover more about yourself since purpose is not a title, one-time event or a hobby. Purpose is realizing who you are and consistently being conscious of allowing it to evolve into every aspect of your life/style. So what is your purpose, your spiritual identity and your mission? I wanted you to catch a glimpse of a process of discovery so you might feel more comfortable initiating your own. You've read about purpose, you're aware of the definitions, hindrances, I'll share some of the benefits and tools of discovery, evolution, creativity and implementation that all lead to certain achievement. It is a conscious act of responsibility for you to count the cost of the journey you are about to take or may already be aware that you are on.

Get Ready

Count the cost. Can you afford not to be you? Even *purpose* works anywhere, all the time and with anybody who will! It pays well internally and externally; spirit, soul and body, and the benefits are eternal… and it guides you on your life's mission. It's you being you, wholeheartedly and will cost you your excuses. Are you ready to give up your excuses? Having a sense of purpose and knowing who you are can cost you every excuse in the book. Excuses that have cost you relationships, joy, financial success, freedom, confidence, caused worry, frustration, stress or a sense of loss. Excuses may have even hampered your God-given ability to enjoy who you are. This is a most exciting time for you! Enjoy the responsibility of creating who you are and who you are becoming! Feel the power of embarking upon an incredible journey. Who you have been is the tool for discovering who you are becoming, on purpose! Get on your mark and ready yourself right now by letting go of fear. It may have been a weird form of comfort, yet an excuse, decide right now to love yourself anyway as you let go. Your unconditional love for you evicts fear from your temple; thoughts and actions. Your spirit, soul and body are where you live. We all get scared sometimes, but don't let fear control you. Most times, it's not that you fear what you can't do, but what you can do; you fear the responsibility of greatness. Let go to love! Decide to do the work, count the cost of the loss with the challenges, the wins and the accomplishments. Either way, you win!

Your Testament: Conduct a cost analysis on what it takes to be you and decide whether not you're ready and willing to pay the price, but you ultimately have the privilege of reaping the benefits. You may even want to make a list of personal hindrances and benefits, pros and cons or sacrifices and payoffs. If you don't know what you have, how can you discover what you need? Count the cost; it tallies in your favor. But, do it for yourself. When it all boils down, if you can take it or leave it, leave it.

Your Testament: What did my cost analysis reveal? What excuses am I ready to stop using? What reasons will I use to achieve?

_____

_____

_____

_____

_____

_____

_____

_____

_____

_____

_____

_____

_____

_____

_____

_____

_____

_____

_____

_____

_____

_____

_____

_____

Be Truthful

This journey is not for those who choose to be strangers to themselves. Be truthful with yourself. There is nothing deep about that, it just makes sense. Why lie to you when you know you are. That's like some kind of weird, double negative thingy. But, you know what? It will still reveal the truth of lying. Admit you don't know who you are, or at least that you'd like to know more about who you are becoming. Tell yourself the truth. Look at your life from inside out with real eyes. If you have been conditioned by negativity, admit it. If you haven't taken advantage of creative opportunities stemming from fear, say it. If you are good at what you do, own it! If you're a TV zombie, gaming junky or any kind of a-holic, deal with it and if need be ask for qualified help! If you don't like who you have become, admit it. If you are happy, show it! If you need to make some serious changes, do it! If you like the way you walk, strut! If you don't like your relationships, fix them! If you love who you are becoming, enjoy it! If you'd like to have a different career, but you are afraid, state it! If you have the best recipe in town, make it! If you want friends, act like it! If you have been in denial or ignorant, decide, admit and learn. Whatever your truth, don't be a stranger to it.

Your Testament: What do I want to do with my life? What does God desire to create through me?

_____

_____

_____

_____

_____

What does it mean to me to be my most authentic self?

_____

_____

_____

_____

What does that look like?

_____

_____

_____

_____

What do I change? How can my life be more affective?

_____

_____

_____

_____

_____

How will discovering my purpose be relevant? To who? How can I make my mission relevant? What is my level of passion? What am I willing to sacrifice?

_____

_____

_____

_____

_____

Who can I count on and who can count on me? How do I form my strategic alliances?

_____

_____

_____

_____

_____

Notice these questions are not about other people. You don't ask purposeful questions and come up with solutions for someone else, purpose is all about you.

Now that is a lot of questions that are not built for shallow or ordinary answers. Again, stop avoiding them. Don't predict your results with limitations. The questions have only seemed difficult because you have previously distanced yourself from them. But now, draw them close and embrace them, they need you as much as you need their solutions. You may even need to ask them out loud. Writing down the answers is the foundation of building your *You Testament*. Even if your best answer is a temporary, "I don't know." At least you now know more of what you don't know and have just created a path of finding out. Writing them down keeps a battle from raging in your mind and deters the thought bully and the pride bully, too. You may not be able to answer right away since that part of you may not trust you to hear the answers and do them. Be patient this is a process not a test. Your genuine answers aren't wrong, but they will evolve. Don't be afraid of the initial discomfort of silence or try to receive your answers hurriedly or competing with the distractions of everyday noise. Your best solutions are birthed when you are quiet and still. You may have to go back to any of these questions after times of relaxation, prayer, meditation or stillness.

Be Still

Stillness has a silent voice that speaks spiritually to atmospheres and situations on the behalf of your humanity. You can put your thoughts on pause and allow the voices of your world to shut up!

They are probably tired of talking and need the rest anyway. Invest in your peace by taking the opportunity to get somewhere, sit down, and be still! Relaxation, prayer and meditation and stillness are available to your life for its overall quality and for the sake of balance and peace. You can do any of these things at anytime, anywhere and you can do them for free. It will only cost you the excuse not to. Even the perception that you have to be religious to pray is unsubstantiated. Or that meditation is only for certain religions. Prayer and meditation can only enhance your spiritual awareness, beliefs and if you decide to follow religious teachings, practices or have those convictions.

There is really no excuse not to be still long enough to relax, pray or meditate. It baffles me when people say they don't have time to do such things. You most certainly have time! If necessary, go back and re-read the hindrances of discovery, most of them are time snatchers or look at your own cost analysis. Balance those areas and you will find all the time you need, plus some, to enjoy the process of being still. It doesn't take long at all. It takes practice, discipline, desire and willingness. But, because they all work out of the Spirit of God which is eternity, they can do more in a few clock minutes than working and hustling can attempt to do all day! The peacefulness, creative ideas, dialogue, mediation, and stillness grant the *shower you* the boldness to emerge.

Your Testament: When will I give myself time be still? What times can I be most consistent?

_____

_____

_____

_____

_____

_____

_____

Relax

Relax. Taking a deep breath can be relaxing enough to recover. Realize you are not in competition with anyone else. And even if for some reason you perceive there is, don't worry about being beat by perceived competition as long as you never lose to yourself. Decide to be more at ease. Reduce severity by discovering ways to loosen up and refresh by upgrading your entertainment. You can start by taking a fifteen-minute nap. It's okay that they aren't exclusively for children. Or just close your eyes (without going to sleep), enjoy being alone or sit in a comfortable chair. Your life may be so noisy that your comfortable chair may be in your car, that's a start. You may like to sip warm tea or a glass of water, or put your feet up, listen to instrumental music that soothes you, pay attention to your breathing, write and smiling all over can be relaxing, too. At least start, and then increase the level of relaxing activity as long as it doesn't invite distracting, mental chatter and busyness. Something like taking a stroll, getting some fresh air, enjoying a little sun, slowly eating a piece of fruit, painting, building a model, gardening, a massage, creative visualization or muscle stretches and grow from there. Relaxing is a way to invite the strategy of balance. Balance is radical and it takes the ingenuity of being still to enjoy time management. Relaxation produces mindfulness, which is being in the now, and not being pestered by the past or you pestering the future. It creates an atmosphere for prayer.

Your Testament: What forms of relaxation work best for me?

_____

_____

_____

_____

_____

_____

_____

_____

_____

_____

Pray

Prayer is taking time to have your most intimate dialogue with God Almighty - *the creative and all sustaining power and connecting life Source for all there is.* It goes beyond the limitations of human communication, yet it expresses your heart to Deity and allows Deity to express to you and is you, too. It's the realization that you are aware, reverent, appreciate and even worship the Spirit of God who is greater than you are, yet is you. Prayer is a time of privileged communication. It's the time where you speak your heart and listen to God's heart for you. It's a two-way! You may enjoy your freedom to use your times of prayer to express appreciation and gratitude, receive direction, and verbalize your most genuine adoration... It's a way to recognize who you are by listening to the Source you're connected to.

Your Testament: How can I make my prayer times more consistent?

_____

_____

_____

_____

_____

_____

_____

_____

_____

_____

_____

_____

_____

_____

_____

_____

_____

_____

_____

_____

_____

Meditate

Meditation is deliberately being quiet for the purpose of slowing your mind down. It can be quite beneficial to your spirit, soul and even your body. According to the Mayo Clinic:

"Meditation is considered a type of mind-body complementary medicine. Meditation produces a deep state of relaxation and a tranquil mind. During meditation, you focus your attention and eliminate the stream of jumbled thoughts that may be crowding your mind and causing stress. This process results in enhanced physical and emotional well-being."

At one time meditation was only associated with Eastern religions or perceived as foreign but, it is easy to disarm ones skepticism about it because for all intents and purposes, it is a simple way to quiet the body and the mind. Meditation is mentally medicinal. It is an invitation of stillness in a very noisy world that can constantly shout demands from every direction. It's like calling an official timeout when stress is lurking, your mind gets tired or your stream of thoughts gets winded. It is putting space between thoughts. There are different ways or approaches to meditation that can appeal to any level of purpose, age, gender, religion, economic status, race or culture. Balance and mindfulness, through meditation can be achieved through being still.

Stillness works on your behalf and has atmospheric conversations, taking your spirit, soul and life places your body will never have to go. Stillness can start with something as simple as writing things down. Have you ever noticed that when you write things down the list is not as long or as loud as your thoughts were yelling it to you? Stillness may appear as if you're not doing anything, but stillness, my friend, is where decisions that can affect your entire life are formed and made.

Implementation: Initial self-discovery begins when you deliberately make time to conduct an *inner-view*, looking into yourself as is, right now. Asking yourself questions that may make you uncomfortable and being willing to receive answers that may cause you to feel vulnerable. It may initially be perceived as selfishness because your questions and answers have a whole lot to do with *me, my and I,* but the solutions will ultimately benefit the world, remember the ripple effect. Picture it by of asking the *shower you* naked, simple, no one around, without titles, labels, brands, obligations or expectations. Don't be afraid to inner-view all of you all the way! As you conduct the inner-view, submit those questions to your three credit reporting agencies: spirit, soul and body and expect them to answer. *Your spirit is that part of you that has no form and does not rely on human substance or tangibility; it is consciousness, a universal connectedness and the force of life that animates your body. It's the incredible power of God, the Source of all that makes your life alive! Your soul is the combination of your emotions, intellectual reasoning, behavioral constructs, personality; it's what characterizes your individuality and makes you unique. Your body is the tangible suit or vehicle that your spirit and soul use to operate within and out of to accomplish missions.*

Be patient, this is a process and it is not a one-time event. You will have the most successful self-discovery when fear doesn't have you, especially of self-exploration and taking a journey within. You have to explore before you can truthfully self-discover! You may even want to decide to enlist or delegate to qualified assistants; spiritual advisor, certified life coach, accountability partner, counselor, therapist, etc.; an achievement team. Conduct your inner-view and while doing so, boldly initiate a DO NOT DISTURB sign, for the entrances of your mind, not just for others, but for you.

Your Testament: What have I written and enjoyed thus far? How am I implementing what's applicable?

_____

_____

_____

_____

_____

_____

_____

_____

_____

_____

_____

_____

_____

_____

_____

_____

Get Set

Be Free

Enjoy the subtle changes it may even feel like a cleansing. If so, wash off some of those most confining labels. You may not want to snatch them off, but through relaxation, prayer, meditation and stillness you can discard, those necessary, a little easier, even if not all the way. At least lift them up a little to see what's underneath. So many things bombard you with labels. Sometimes, in trying to answer the question of who you are, the answer may more easily be revealed in stating who you are not. Everything from the media, the internet, fashion, titles, duties, functions, race, religion, social ties, etc. has done an outstanding job to get us to buy into labels that have buried our identity like successful undertakers. Again, it doesn't mean labels are wrong; they identify items, manufacturers and the designers that can be used to decorate who we are, but those labels do not completely define you, but they do provide categorical descriptions and relationship's architectural definitions. Be free to dry the *shower you* off and allow yourself to emerge. Be honest and deny hypocrisy. It's not that you should never be critical or judge, there is great wisdom in critical thinking. You do have the right and responsibility to assess the internal and external situations, but how you judge is the same criteria by which you will be judged and criticized. So even when it comes to you, hold off on hypocrisy and harsh judgment. Be free! Just remember while freedom reigns, discipline holds the mirror!

Acceptance

Accept the great ideals about God you may not have had before, choose to think differently. When you find yourself in an old thought pattern, change your mind. Decide to be you, even if you don't know all the details of who that is; it will come and spiritual maturity will form as you implement. Be free to re-create and re-define. Be free to accept yourself as is, even if there is a level of uncertainty of where to place your foot outside the box. Decide to love yourself unconditionally and be completely accepting of who you are, yet open to purpose to discover even better.

Your Testament: Define freedom. Am I free? What would it take for me to experience true freedom? Do I accept who I am? What would it take for me to accept myself unconditionally?

_____

_____

_____

_____

_____

_____

_____

_____

_____

_____

_____

It's Your Turn!

_____

_____

_____

_____

_____

_____

_____

_____

_____

_____

_____

_____

_____

_____

_____

_____

_____

_____

_____

_____

_____

_____

_____

_____

_____

_____

Let's Go!

Your Testament: Implementation: If you've read, answered the questions, created your own questions and answered them, and have done the work of implementation thus far, you've probably already discovered who you are – your purpose. If you have, say so! Absolutely! Maybe you skimmed through the pages to get to this point to get right to it. If you worked, discovery will, too. If you hit and missed or skimmed, discovery will skim right over you, too. You will get out of it exactly what you put into it. If you have been doing the work, this won't take long because you've implemented parts of this process along the way already. Either way, welcome to you! Welcome to your purpose, the identifiable awareness of God in you! Enjoy this simple process of self-discovery to continue to reveal your purpose:

1. Set a date and time to be alone and quiet. Fifteen to thirty minutes, but everyone is different so let time tell you how much of you it needs.

2. Make sure you have taken care of natural urges like hunger and thirst or even the restroom.

3. Make sure the environment is as quiet as possible; even the ticking of a watch can be distracting.

4. Sit comfortably and relax.

5. Think about who you are beyond names, labels, responsibilities—all of them and relax without carrying that weight. What may feel like emptiness is weightlessness.

6. Pay attention to your breathing and breathe deliberately, deeply and slowly; throughout this process.

7. Enjoy the experience of not having to do or be anything.

8. Let the mental chatter cease and any mental pictures fade until they go blank.

9. Feel the presence of God that has always been there and accept it by being conscious of it and allowing it to intensify naturally.

10. Without hypocrisy or second-guessing, begin to verbalize what you are feeling, thinking or experiencing, whisper it if you have to, and write it down. Say it; repeat it out loud even if it feels a little strange.

Write down the date and time, too. Don't discount or search for reason, but do the process again if you need to. It's a process to get used to doing anyway. You should be able to experience a great degree of satisfaction about this discovery even if it spawns exciting questions. Enjoy this initial answer to begin with, there is more to follow...

Your Testament: Who am I and what is my purpose?

_____

_____

_____

_____

_____

_____

_____

_____

_____

_____

_____

_____

_____

_____

Now is perfect time to use wisdom to get your achievement team together for the sake of building relationships, maturity and accountability. Accept the authentic presence of God that you are and enjoy a new way of being. If you find yourself to be resistant to self-acceptance and the process of discovery, at least decide to come away with a different perception even an ability to be more accepting of others. Celebrate your discovery! You are enough! Enjoy the benefits!

Your Testament: What did I discover? How was the experience? How do I feel? What are my thoughts?

_____

_____

_____

_____

_____

_____

_____

_____

_____

_____

_____

_____

_____

_____

Your testament: How can my purpose support my current mission? How will it serve the vision of my plans for future mission(s)?

_____

_____

_____

_____

_____

_____

_____

_____

_____

_____

_____

_____

_____

_____

_____

_____

_____

Purpose is now working full-time and wants you to take full advantage of your complete benefits package. Let the benefits begin! Solutions! Solutions! Solutions! The benefits are endless and reveal solutions. Knowing your purpose and consistently living from your spiritual identity is powerful. It is also attractive, fun, exciting and intriguing. It's like the whole world is an orchestra and you know how to blend harmoniously; yet like a prodigy who understands your instrument, your solos keep getting encore after encore!! YOU are the greatest benefactor, then so goes the harmony in the ripple effect. It's good to know your purpose, but it only becomes incredibly amazing when you activate the essence of your spiritual identity. Purpose gives your life meaning now, your life's mission is clearer and well established, and it requires your beliefs to be supportive, your relationships to be healthy and purposeful. Starting with the one you have with yourself, joy and happiness will be consistent, you can maintain an overall healthy lifestyle and create sustaining wealth conducive for your life. You can create a productive reality rather than having a form of reality fed to you by ill-fitting opinion, persuasive media, archaic assumptions or the herd-like movement of society's unfulfilling routines. You come alive! Your sensitivity heightens; you become wide-awake, conscious of all the wonderful things within and around you. Your visions and dreams are in real-time with your reality and not some random fantasy or wishful thinking. It's not a fairy tale, it is the story of your life and every day you realize you are making history! What history will you make today? That's what purpose will do for you! Again, it's not about grinning all the time like the people on the *Orbit* gum commercial or being some creampuff or a pushover. Again, purpose doesn't discount aggression, anger, a *bad* attitude, unhappiness, displeasure, frustration, annoyance and the like. Purpose can use the wisdom of passion to deploy those things as tools for your mission, but they won't control you! Instead of you walking around name-dropping, purpose will drop your name. Your decision-making becomes precise and you take pleasure in your divine consciousness. You become more focused, empowered, and energized by passion. You realize that who you are matters and what you do is relevant.

Your Testament: What solutions do I need right now? What history would I like to create? What are my thoughts and feelings? Create questions and answers.

_____

_____

_____

_____

_____

_____

Chapter Seven

BENEFITS OF DISCOVERY

BENEFITS OF DISCOVERY

Discovery

Self-Discovery

This part of your discovery is only the beginning, but self-discovery is a lifestyle, it's a continuum. When you know who you are, it allows everything in you to become more clearly defined and natural alignment occurs. Self-discovery is not a one-time endeavor, but a way of life that allows you to experience continual advancement in every area of your life. It allows you to realize your thoughts and dreams are only controlled by the limitations you set for them. It facilitates the environment for you to awaken to your life's purpose and enjoy living it out loud. Self-discovery can use transition as a tool to take down some of the windows that have become distracting so you can put up a mirror. The mirror is not an opportunity to become selfish or narcissistic, but to conduct the research of your lifetime in order for you to be mindful to give your best presentation. You can't control the perception, but you can enjoy the responsibility of producing a most excellent demonstration.

Self-discovery becomes contagious because as you commit to do the work of self-discovery everything else in your life begins to wake up and find its place, too, including people. It does take discipline, but it's not toil, its *light* work, it's enlightening, enriching and empowering. You stop depleting your energy caused by reaching out to *find yourself* and you begin to refuel by reaching within to discover that the treasure of God that has always been you births passion.

Rest easy, discovery is to connect or reconnect with something that's already there. When people go on a quest or hunt to discover treasure, the treasure already exists. The desire to know the treasure, its worth and the awareness of its existence just has to be acknowledged and unearthed. The treasure of your purpose is already within you! God is! You are certainly becoming more aware of it and reconnecting with it. So what you are reaching for, you already are! Self-discovery is just a conscious process of self-acceptance and authenticity and the continual development of your greatest self. Self-discovery allows you to see who you are, and that purpose is enough! Purpose is not reaching out and finding yourself, or who you are, but accepting who you already are within and realizing you are enough! So, "Bring your whole mind with you and do the work!"

I remember when I was a freshman entering college I thought I had be like the college girls on the show *A Different World*. Talk about the effects of been so influenced by entertainment. Back in 1987-1989, the cast of the show had the fashion sense that oozed being eclectic, confident, hip and independent. They were smart, funny, creative, and their problems got solved in thirty minutes. So I thought I had to have the right asymmetrical hairstyle, their body shape, be popular, hang out and have the perfect college male friend who only wanted to walk me to class, go with me to events where folks were coupled off and kiss…just kiss. I thought I had to have good camaraderie with the dorm matron, the RA's, the folks in the cafeteria and my professors like they did. Remember Kimberly Reese and Mr. Gaines being buddies? I wanted the grades and everything else that looked like a hip college student. It seemed like a lot of pressure to live up to what I thought a college freshman at an HBCU would look like and I knew I didn't have what it took.

I didn't have the money to buy the clothes, my parents and home life was not like the Huxtables. I didn't have the swag or the willingness to give up what I liked about myself to attempt to be popular. I didn't even know how to be popular. I wasn't at all popular in high school, so no need to cram for it now. I lacked the discipline it took to get and maintain a GPA worth bragging about. Truth be told, I wasn't one who was into fashion. I liked my hair the way it was, I could do it myself and it looked very nice, I was satisfied with my small waist and big thighs & hips in spite of smaller girls who could get boyfriends. I didn't have a boyfriend in high school and college was no different. Some of my good friends were guys so I was never really impressed by boys or men romantically and I didn't want the headache of having to fend off more than a kiss. Nor did I want to be the subject of some of the *boy's locker room conversations* I had become privy to. I didn't like to go out and it seemed like such a chore to do my hair, put on make-up and clothes only to get all sweaty from dancing or be the dreaded wallflower. Those appropriate club clothes and heels were so uncomfortable and I didn't think a young man's compliments, or not would be worth my discomfort.

I wasn't at all like those girls I saw on TV or most of the ones who were on my college campus. There were a couple of friendships I made back then that are still viable today. One of them inspired me to write this book. We wore just a little hint of misfit. But, at that time, my young mind was whipped by my ignorant expectations and innocent perceptions of their impressions. My self-induced pressure made the peer pressure look like a punk and both pressures felt overwhelming before I even went to my college orientation. I had level of support at home and I believe my parents supported me the best they knew how. But, their support was energized by a level of Christianity that wasn't conducive for the environment I was venturing into. It didn't match the level of support I thought I needed, yet I was able to maintain most of those values when they were nowhere around for my relationship with God had developed my own values, convictions and thought-provoking questions. But, the possible rejection of not being able to be obedient to them and the perception of Godliness they instilled in me was so overwhelming; I almost did not go to college that year. I was more worried about finding a church than I was about finding my class. I was afraid of not being who I saw on TV and what other students who went to college a year or so before seemed to have successfully become. The weight of my own expectations was sickening, literally. It was too much to reach for. But I went on to Winston Salem State University anyway…

One day, within the first few weeks of school and during my voice class, my professor spoke words that would shift the perception of my life. She was talking about what it would take to succeed in her class, be a good student, a good freshman and graduate. I had the good student and the good freshman part down, but I must not have wanted to be a graduate because I didn't. She didn't talk long and she seemed to want to get to the singing part of the class, and I wanted her to, too! But, she talked about not having to do what you think it takes to fit in and she said, *"Whatever a freshman is, you already are because you are here! You made it in, you made it here! Whatever it takes to be a voice student you already are because you are in this class, now just do the work! Bring your whole mind with you and just do the work!"* Those words rang in my ear and throughout the corridors of my entire life. I felt like she was only talking to me forever. Those words caused me to appreciate being different and create a new and very positive perception of myself. I wrote them down. I read them daily for a while until I began to know: Whatever I am a freshman is! I felt empowered to shape the definition into what I wanted it to be. I was able to see that I had the power to become the definition and the personification of anything I decided to be. I could make it look bad or I could make it feel so right to me in a way that would positively affect others. It wasn't about the girls I saw on TV, the stereotypes, expectations of my parents, and the resistance of being a negative statistic, the confines of religion, and all the students on campus or societal ideals. That day, at eighteen years old, I decided to live from principle: what I am reaching for, I already am, just bring my whole mind with me and do the work! That experience helped intensify the expanse and rate of all my questions, too. I realized that day that I didn't have to succumb to self-induced nor external pressures to be what I already was. I was *me* first! I was a college student. I was a freshman; I was in her voice class. I realized that the *purpose* for me being there was already being fulfilled simply because I showed up! I had to discover I was enough regardless! I didn't have to be like anyone else or allow stereotypes, statics and generalizations to define me; mine or anyone else's. No matter what preconceived ideas or ideals have been, I had the God-given privilege and responsibility to incorporate them, change them, and let them expire or just go away.

Your Testament: What about me? What am I reaching for that I already am? What definitions or labels am I trying to live up to? How will I bring my whole mind with me? How can I commit to do the work? How can I decide I don't have to fulfill anyone else's assumed expectations or ill-fitting definitions to be who I am or become all I want to be?

_____

_____

_____

_____

_____

_____

_____

_____

_____

_____

_____

_____

_____

_____

_____

_____

_____

_____

_____

_____

_____

_____

_____

_____

_____

Once you begin to live your decisions, you become the definition. For me, that was an introduction to a greater level of inner peace that defied my own common sense. The pressure was off! Peace emerges. The benefits of knowing who you are incorporate a sustaining peace into your life. Some live such lives of chaos where peace seems boring. It's not a fairytale peace where there are no troubles or sorrows, but the peace of being able to see chaos and problematic issues and know they are dead already! *That* peace trumps everyday understanding! Contentment in spite of! The benefits of knowing who you are, are infinite and the positive ripple effect is immeasurable. Knowing your purpose offers you the benefits that will set you on a progressive path to discover, evolve, create, implement and achieve continually.

Self-discovery is the energy of natural alignment and balance. Self-discovery isn't a time when you begin to think so much of yourself that it invites selfishness or arrogance. It is an intentional process of realizing who you are so that you and everyone you are connected to knows who they are getting. Some people would rather lazily accept an imposed social assignment, external contouring or, like a parasite, exist dependent on the identity of another rather than do the work of discovering their own. That's dysfunction's playhouse. Self-discovery is the privilege and responsibility to see that all roads lead back to God in you, *the creative and all sustaining power and connecting life Source for all there is,* your purpose. It takes a copious amount of courage to initiate self-discovery, mainly because you have to admit you don't know your purpose or aren't familiar enough with who you are to live it consistently or effectively. You have to bring your whole mind in, yourself, and do the work! Admittance is the hard work, but discovering your purpose, as you have experienced, is so rewarding and offers you the consistent satisfaction of completely being your greatest self. You can experience self-discovery in or out of religion because who you are IS no matter what set of beliefs, values and practices of a spiritual leader you chose. If you don't believe me stop practicing and believing religiously for just a moment; if you dare, and see if you ain't, *still is*. I know that's bad grammar, but it's positively beneficial! You can exist out of it, in it, through it and beyond it.

Self-discovery can enhance your religious experience and in other cases, religion may not be a conduit for discovery. Some may use it to become aware of godliness and a level spirituality. Religion can be a catalyst, but don't use it as an excuse not to pursue spiritual intelligence. Some religious habits seem to have conditioned folks to leave their spiritual intelligence at home or in the parking lot, while they go in to worship a human who claims to be a much better representation of God's image than they are. If religion is improperly used, it can breed self-ignorance, spiritual exploitation and become a type of modern day mental and physical enslavement.

Churches and some religious customs at their best can be wonderful ways to connect with people of like purpose, who collectively intensify the awareness of God and use tradition as a way to promote the truth and the progression of spirituality. If it is ever used as a substitute or prerequisite for the accountability of you knowing and living your spiritual essence of the God in you, your life will perpetuate the very dysfunction the tenets of spirituality abhors. Throughout your self-discovery, you can also unearth the great truths of your religious expression and take the opportunity to see positive similarities in the religious perceptions of others. Knowing what you believe and at least attempting to understand the beliefs of others makes conditions ripe for unity, instead of using religion as a tool for hate or segregation. Its man's varied perceptions of God that produces the separatisms called religion, but God knows God is ONE! Some religions specifically promote division (us versus them, this way or no way), prejudice (race and gender) and arrogance (the usurping power in titles and position) which can completely reject love (the ONE who God is) for all humanity (what you are), diversity (the unique quality of who you are meant to be) and unity (the ultimate, Divine Spirit of who we are collectively). Require your beliefs to answer you! Rest assured the Omnipotent, Omnipresent, Omniscient Spirit Source of all God is, is magnificent enough to handle your thoughts and questions about anything, including the divine discovery of you purpose. Self-Discovery is the game changer that promotes questions and solutions that balance the spiritual playing field, even via religion. It promotes self-responsibility and illuminates your individual path and guides in the direction of other like minds and if that is a healthy religious experience, so be it! We are all of one

Spirit designed to experience life via means of infinite expressions. That's incredible! Discovering your purpose is revealing your unique expression and spiritual identity to you and others.

Your Testament: Describe your thoughts and feelings. Create questions, answers and make practical application.

_____

_____

_____

_____

_____

_____

_____

_____

_____

_____

_____

_____

_____

_____

_____

_____

_____

_____

_____

_____

_____

_____

Evolve

As self-discovery increases consciousness and spiritual intelligence so does your ability to evolve. Sometimes traditions, hindrances of discovery and religion can retard your spiritual intelligence and stagnation can set in. You may have allowed those things to dull your own ability to reason or provide meaning. They have the ability to make you lazy and not exercise your innate, working knowledge or engage passion. You may be able to use tradition or religion to help you, but with or without, you have to decide to change, evolve and discover you. Purpose will allow you to use your life in its highest form and greatest potential evidential through evolution. When you know who you are things around you become more clearly defined and you begin to be more sensitive to your quality of reasoning. Evolving is a process as well and it begins by seeing the need to. Evolve means to develop and achieve gradually. It's also being aware of the gradual development. Gradual does not have to mean slow it's just a consistency of progression. So to make a deliberate, conscious and continual effort to evolve takes place through gradual stages, decisions, changes, growth, recreating and redefining.

Your Testament: How am I already evolving?

_____

_____

_____

_____

_____

_____

_____

_____

_____

_____

_____

_____

_____

_____

_____

_____

Decisions

Your purpose will require the privilege of strategic decision making, the beginning of which will be revealed as you conduct your inner-views of self-discovery. You have to decide *to do* before you decide what to do. Knowing your purpose will not only help you make decisions, but self-discovery allows you to become the decisions you make. I remember when I was so uncomfortable and unfulfilled with my career path. I knew that my purpose and mission were beyond what my humanity was experiencing at the time. I would charge very little, volunteer to coach (vocal, career, spirituality and life) and coach people pro bono and sometimes I coached people without them realizing what I was doing. I knew something about helping people discover who they are, and their tailored solutions were part of my life's mission. I love it and I'm better than good at it! I also knew it wasn't something I could jump right into, have a legitimate profession and say, "Tah dah!! Step right up!" I knew becoming a certified life coach (specializing in self-discovery and relationships), a spiritual life strategist, speaker, advisor and author answered some of my mission questions. I knew I had the gift, my purpose and passion supported it. But, I wanted to do everything I knew to legitimize the mission to those who didn't know, but need to. My beliefs, the balance of the example teachings of Christ and experiences, hurts, spiritual knowledge, dysfunction, hand-picked labels, church and community involvement, imperfections, personality, professional endeavors and career paths; all had to make sense and mature my impassioned mission(s). I set some goals and made a plan.

I decided to finish school and earn my degree in Behavioral Science and I knew I wanted a reputable coaching certification and life strategy would follow suit. I had the evidence now I just wanted to bring down the gavel! The decision to do them and by the grace of God I became them. I became the graduate and I became the certified coach, master life strategist, speaker, facilitator, author, etc. I didn't do it alone and it took some time, but I knew what I loved to do, versus what I was good at and being paid to do where two different things. I had good jobs, great employers in times past, and steady income over a twenty-six-year time frame. But, the last job I was hired for...Oh my goodness! There were days I hated to go to work. I was physically ill during most of my five-year tenure. But, I didn't quit when I wanted to.

I needed a paycheck and I needed keep the health insurance I was beginning to have to use. I also knew there were lessons for me to learn for the next phase of my life. One of them was: How NOT to treat people. I had a front row seat! Another lesson was: Self-ignorance is toxic and can be infectious. Those two lessons alone intensified my passion. I also learned how purpose would pay you in a wealth that money can't buy! At that particular place of employment, my duties were somewhat fulfilling, yet robotic and mundane, I liked my peers, but management was horrible, no advancement opportunities, training or support, the pay was a joke and an overall archaic environment made going to work most days seem like working in hell's basement—dark, heated chaos. The God in me, my purpose, set the goals and created the plan. The confidence in purpose allowed me to make the decision, take my coaching service full-time, for the first time. My previous realizations of being enough gave me the assurance that I'd be enough for this, too. When enough is enough, it is!

Your Testament: What are a few of my greatest lessons? What does enough mean to me?

_____

_____

_____

_____

_____

_____

_____

_____

_____

_____

_____

_____

_____

_____

_____

_____

In 2005, my extended family fell apart, I was very ill, had recently relocated from Okinawa, Japan, new job, funny money, strained relationships, distant friends, etc.; I had to coach myself full-time and others in the midst of life-changing trials. I always had, but this time, I was fully aware my next mission heavily depended upon it. I learned so much about what I don't know. The more I learned the more intimidated I got. But, I had purpose, mission, passion, my testament and I had so much to implement. I was stoked! It was more than words written it was a lesson plan and guide for strategic achievement. I knew the process could involve patience, sacrifice and work, but I didn't think that other job I was hired for that felt like working on a chain gang would be a part of it. I had to get in my place, a place of peace! I needed Peace Place. I had made the decision to execute my mission(s), but I didn't realize, my experience at that job taught me some things in order for the decision to *make* me. I didn't want to run; I wanted to build a place of peace right in the midst of it! I consciously chose to continue to evolve. I had to become the decision purpose made. During that time I saw single parents mistreated and couldn't leave, seeing they had to provide for their children, managers and supervisors sabotage the employee's efforts for betterment, I saw people who didn't think they could do any better; I saw other people become sick with stress in an environment that withheld the cure. But, I witnessed and experienced the power of evolution; determination, purposeful decision-making, betterment breakthroughs, the will to try and see it pay off. Most of all the healing properties of laughter is always good medicine and has perpetual side effects. I knew my purpose and the mission I wanted to accomplish before I worked there, but I learned so many things that enriched my life forever and enhanced the decisions that made me.

I had a series of evolutions. I quit college years ago and had to finish earning my degree full-time, and get my coaching certifications while working full-time and coaching clients on the side whenever I could find a side. Passion was in full affect. I knew it was purposeful because the energy wasn't stressful or ripping my immediate family apart, but it created a passion that drew us closer together and initiated new fulfillment and discoveries. It was a gradual evolution for me to go from deciding to being. I became my decision and the evolution allowed the decision to become me. I was fully aware of evolving and I wanted to; needed to. The quality of my life depended on it. Your evolutions may take place in an entirely different time frame or situations, but either way, a keen sense decision making comes into play as you are in the stages of evolving. Consciously decide, set goals, plan, achieve and evolve. I evolved, which allowed me change on purpose—missions accomplished! There's more to come, you, too!

Your Testament: What decisions can I make? What decisions can make me? How can I evolve? What does my mission look like?

_____

_____

_____

_____

_____

_____

_____

_____

_____

_____

_____

_____

_____

_____

_____

_____

_____

_____

_____

_____

_____

_____

Change

One change makes room for another. The word change means to be different, transform, modify, exchange or switch. Be different! You already are different so embrace your uniqueness! Forgive my slang, but normal don't know nobody and different has everybody's name. Accept your being different as God's way of choosing to live as only God can through you. To do that you may have to change your mindset and your lifestyle and understand that it's not just a one-time thing. You've changed since the day you were born, went to school or had you first whatever or whomever. You already know change is constant and inevitable, but as you evolve and realize your purpose, you will initiate changes instead of being forced by them. As your desire to change evolves, you will set a course that will allow you to use the desire of change as a tool. As you change, you are aware that the change changes you! That's the benefit of purpose. This is about you seeing who you are and accepting all that is, not an audition for a show. This will allow you to have undisputable evidence of marked growth for yourself.

Your Testament: What can I change now? How do I want to change? What do I need to do to implement the change? How can I maintain the changes I make?

_____

_____

_____

_____

_____

_____

_____

_____

_____

_____

_____

_____

_____

_____

_____

_____

_____

_____

_____

_____

_____

_____

_____

_____

_____

_____

_____

_____

_____

Growth

You know, growth means to expand, gain, increase in amount, develop and reach maturity. Your awareness of growth, personally and professional is the support to continue. Isn't it something how you expect and even command for children to grow and mature, but you allow yourself so much slack. Sure children have a faster rate of physical growth, but they are expected to learn at school and go home and do homework, get tested and pass, survive peer pressure, bullying, emerge through puberty, ignore negative influence and not talk to strangers! This supposedly proves discipline and growth. They also ask a lot of questions, too. Children learn a great deal with their eyes and maybe they are being taught how to allow people to command things of them, and when they grow up to be adults they won't have to continually mature or require advancement from themselves. They see some adults go straight home from work frustrated by jobs they don't like and do nothing more than the same old mundane things day in and day out. Get up, commute, get to work, go to lunch, leave work, commute, go home, get on the computer, watch TV and go to bed just to do it all over again. Oh wait, I can't forget those who are advanced and go work out, go to church or religious meetings, social events, hit the grocery store and take the kids to practice or watch a game. That's high quality redundant right there. Is this what our youth should work hard to become? What life class are you teaching them? Don't get me wrong there are habits you choose to develop that are necessary for day-to-day functions to have structure, balance and some predictability to produce stability and accountability. But, if those habits have become so mundane that they frustrate your dreams, goals and innate desire of fulfillment, you are stagnant. Stagnation knows there *has got* to be more to life than this, but it doesn't feel empowered to do anything about it. Stagnation begins to decay everything around it. It also promotes the assumption that someone else will pick up the slack for advancement. But, purpose is restorative. It facilitates growth, begins to align your entire being, and creates a pattern of movement that expands to every area of your life. Even if there is an initial push back, it eventually supports your purposed rhythm and increases development and maturity. That development or growth may spark a much needed paradigm shift.

A shift in who you are can initiate the benefits of purpose, but it offers prime opportunities to recreate and redefine who you are to yourself and eventually to others. The process of self-discovery is all about YOU! You can't remove unbecoming labels and titles as long as you are continuing to live up to them. What they ignorantly called you and what you may have called yourself can end its course with a decision, backed up by a lifestyle. *Let me restate, you are not what happened to you or what you've done—good, bad or indifferent nor are you just the one who lived through it, but you ARE the one who knew you would!* The benefit of redefining who you are comes with a truckload of responsibility yet purpose completely supports the privilege for you to do so every step of the way. Don't run from the idea of responsibility, it's yours whether you accept it or not. So, go ahead and decide in advance to enjoy the privileges of having the responsibility to grow.

Your Testament: Who am I, now? What more do I want to become? What else can I do with my life? How can I grow? How can I be held accountable to grow? How else can I carry out my purpose?

_____

_____

_____

_____

_____

_____

_____

_____

_____

_____

_____

_____

_____

_____

_____

_____

_____

_____

_____

_____

_____

_____

Checking in with those three credit-reporting agencies (spirit, soul and body) I talked about earlier will answer those questions, giving you supportive report. Even if the report, your spiritual assessment, doesn't change your purpose, what it can reveal is instruction for execution that will be deliberate, mindful and strategic. It may even lead to establishing purposeful relationships.

Your Testament: What am I discovering, thinking and feeling? What am I doing about it? How well do I do it? What purposeful relationships can I solidify or establish?

_____

_____

_____

_____

_____

_____

_____

_____

_____

_____

_____

_____

_____

_____

_____

_____

_____

_____

_____

_____

_____

_____

Create

The ability to create can be so underrated. It is the ability to take something from spirit into existence or awareness. How awesome is that! Purpose allows you to create and provide for your own existence because you realize your existence goes beyond your physical form so you thrive from greater. You realize who you are, is enough for what you do. The benefits of purpose may involve removing dysfunction from a relationship or changing the relationship. It may cost you some relationships, personal and professional, but you won't have to force it. Your purpose, mission and passion will cause it to level out for you when you decide to be truthful, be still, be free, be mindful, be conscious, and be ready! Purpose enhances that realization by starting with your thought life, which is your ability to create thought.

Creative thoughts are absolutely beneficial to your spiritual expression and your human experience. Your thoughts are only hindered by the limitations you assign to them. Your thoughts can't create what you don't believe and won't violate the willingness of your behavior. So much of what you have or don't have in your life is because you created it by thinking or not. Look within and look around. If your thoughts are constant victims of the *thought bully*, creative ideas may be a flash in the pan. And your purpose-induced thoughts are victimized before they ever knew you loved them or their possibilities. Purpose and self-discovery give you the courage to stop bullying your mind with so much negative thought of self. The love you have for yourself and how you think about yourself is contagious. When you are enough for yourself, you emanate that satisfaction to all of your influences. Your creative thoughts are the evidence of how you feel about yourself and your life and the foundation your other relationships build upon. Your thoughts are the place where everything that makes up your essence convenes; they are where the *shower you* lives and should never be afraid to be alone with you. You create why beautiful things can happen and do them or you can spout off the hindrances and give those things reason to die. Your thoughts are not you, but you are the one who creates them. That's why thinking alone is insufficient, but quieting your thoughts, meditatively is quite beneficial for direction. But, if I asked you to imagine or think of a pink elephant inside a white picket fence, by request, you can create the thought, but you are neither the elephant nor the white, picket fence. You are separate from your thoughts, but your life tattle tales on them. More than *you are what you eat*, but your life becomes what you think…or not!

Creativity doesn't just exist in your thought life, but that's where your blueprints and instruction manuals begin. Your divine, creative thoughts are filled with the greatness of incredible possibilities. But, it's no longer satisfying for you to know them simply for the sake of information, like knowing there is a moon. They also deserve more than to be held hostage by fears your ignorant-self introduce to your mind. It would also be most beneficial if you stop giving fear and worry your ideas. Most tormenting ideas you give your best thoughts; worry, never happens. Use your creative energy to make your *what ifs* positive. Not that you live a life full of wild-flower meadows, and you must engage wisdom, but there is already enough perceived negativity, why add to it via thought?

Your Testament: What are some of my greatest thoughts and most valued ideas?

_____

_____

_____

_____

_____

_____

_____

_____

_____

_____

_____

_____

_____

_____

_____

_____

_____

_____

_____

_____

_____

Purpose offers you the benefits of thinking about possibilities and creating new things including mental processes and perceptions that will be advantageous. Even when it comes to what you think other people are saying, they usually aren't. Don't flatter yourself; most people aren't thinking that way about you at all. The few who may be aren't thinking of you that long to be as creative as your thoughts are of what you think they may think! It's enough to think for your own life, don't take your thoughts to a swap meet that no one else is showing up for. Free yourself, it's not much about what they think anyway; it's about what you believe and live. Once you own your privilege of creating the energy of a divine thought life, your thoughts will be so positively powerful they will have to live. The life of your ability to create purpose-filled thoughts will be appreciated by the actions they produce and the experiences they become. Thoughts are your creativity's planning department. What you think about something; your mental perception is crucial. Please don't think they don't matter.

Because creativity is such an incredible tool and benefit for purpose and your thoughts are the tool room, it would be even more beneficial to initiate mind renewal and spiritual cleansing. Meditation is a great place to start. Relaxation, prayer, meditation, stillness, reading and implementing self-help aids can also provide a sense of perpetual mind renewal. Be sure to allow it all to flow through purpose and accountability. It should be refreshing and a healthy cleansing of your mind, not brainwash. Purpose will allow wisdom to develop your criteria and ensure balance. Your thought life gets you in touch with you and then you animate it by touching the world. The ability to create goes way beyond thought. There are aspects of what you create that can be felt and seen. And in order to allow the power of your creative thought to be seen, you don't just think them, but use them. You may have allowed fear to grip a newborn thought that has become DOA or stagnant. Don't think yourself stagnant because that requires creativity and energy, too! There is a difference between *being still* and *stuck*! Allow your creative thoughts to directly and deliberately reflect in your actions, resuscitate those thoughts. Remember, your purpose allows your mind to enjoy witnessing the creative behavior of its maturing, using the evidence of action.

Your Testament: When was I most creative? How can I be creative now? What will I do with my creativity? How can I be accountable to be creative?

_____

_____

_____

_____

_____

_____

_____

_____

_____

_____

_____

Implement

You don't buy a cookbook just to look at the pictures of the food, read the recipes and then eat the paper. You bought the cookbook for the purpose of cooking something and eating. You see what recipes you like, look at the ingredients, go shopping for what you may not have, read the instructions, incorporate all the tools you need to get the job done and then you eat! Even if yours doesn't look like the picture, you made it. Even if the taste isn't quite right, it's better than eating pages. The best way not to forget a thought or principle is to live it. Knowledge lived is impossible to forget, especially on purpose. It is a wonderful privilege to be a trusted conduit for Spirit to flow into existence; it's a benefit of purpose. It's the pleasure of royalty! You can read this book of purpose, any self-help book, positive social media, the newspaper or even your sacred, religious textbook from cover to cover and it won't change a thing if you don't implement what you read. Learn the importance of living the applicable principles and information. The lack of implementation can frustrate the hell out of you because it supports division. If your mind knows one thing, but your life isn't living it out and, in some cases, it's afraid to, that conflict causes stress. Stress is when the internal is inconsistent with the external. Some of the stress you may be going through has very little to do with other people, but the fact that what you know and what you do are infighting. In order to use any self-help tool you must implement, do the work to execute your spiritual policy. Help yourself! It's not difficult to allow an example to come to mind. I know there are some schools of thought that say faith is all you need or *just pray about it*. That may be needful and to some degree helpful sometimes, but even faith requires work. Purpose may allow your prayers to be answered by the use of your brilliant mind and creative hands. Faith won't come to the job if work doesn't show up first.

Implementation isn't merely for deeds worthy of the Pulitzer Prize. It starts with the little things that are a part of daily life. For instance, my weight has gone up and down most of my adult life, mostly up. It isn't magic; it's due to the lack of implementation. I think I can gain three pounds overnight by drinking water and breathing air. Like most people, I know exactly what it takes to lose weight and keep it off: eat healthy and exercise regularly. I know there are good carbs and bad carbs, I know I could eat more fruits and vegetables and I know apple pie doesn't count as a fruit and potato chips don't count as a vegetable, right? I know I should do more cardio as well as strength train. Most people know these things. I could eat a more balanced diet and with bad knees or not I could exercise more consistently. I haven't implemented the knowledge consistently, so it can become what I do instead of being something I think I should do. Remember the Tae Bo work out videos? Well, I remember one time I was with a friend and I bought the VHS set (a long time ago, eh?!) and we planned for her to come over so we could do the Tae Bo workout together. Well, she came over, we warmed up with Billy Blanks, and then, my phone rang. I answered and after I ended the very short telephone conversation, she and I started talking about the video. I offered her some tea and well…what started out as us drinking water and warming up had progressed to sweet tea, her chicken salad, chips, snacks and sitting down. All we did was *watch* Billy and the crew. We warmed up and cooled down all at the same time. We didn't implement a thing and it showed! Have you ever been so out of shape that your clothes get frustrated? Frustrated clothes roll up, gap, gather, pinch and pull! I mean it's a terrible thing to have your girdle and knee highs roll down at the same time. It'll change your walk and have you walking sideways. Well, our ill-fitting clothes were so frustrated with us and we were frustrated with ourselves. We wore our frustrated Sunday suits, but were thankful that our expanding frames would be hidden underneath our choir robes. We evolved into a life of elastic waistbands or as she said, "Rubber in the waist." We had the workout clothes, TV, VCR, the video, time and space, but we didn't use it. Poor Billy was trying to help us, but the only thing we helped ourselves to was talking, eating and drinking which allowed us to need plenty of rubber in the waist. We knew, but we didn't do. We did not implement. I never did workout right to those tapes. I wonder if she still makes her homemade chicken salad…

You can probably think of some things that are funny and not so funny in your life where you knew, but you didn't do. Purpose has a way of merging your thinking with doing until they become one and the same. Purposeful implementation authorizes you to benefit from your reality being punctual to what your spirit and soul hire it to do. As you exercise the benefit of implementation, it increases your ability because the things you put into practical application that bless your life will be contagious. Once you accomplish one task, it's a stepping-stone to another. Implementation develops the ability to become more purposeful and impassioned about what you say by becoming what you do. You go from *I think I can do it* to *I'm doing it* right into *I did it!*

Achieve

To achieve means to experience a successful conclusion or to implement a task and carry it out victoriously. Have you ever started something that you still haven't finished? You may have started out with a strategic plan and great energy. But, something happened; maybe the money ran out, wrong motives, it took so long you lost interest, or maybe it was a matter of time, etc. To start something and just stop can be quite frustrating, daunting, and costly especially if you aren't able to experience a successful conclusion at any level. Habits of incompletion make perceived failure more palatable with each occurrence. Be it reading or writing a book, remodeling, going school, various forms of self-improvement, planting a garden or promising to do something for or with someone, the pill of disappointment gets easier to swallow.

Your intentions may be great, but what makes it fizzle out is being disconnected from purpose. Purpose shapes the project from start to finish—from discovery to achievement. The benefit of an activated purpose converts the self-ignorant and creates employment opportunities for achievement.

Your Testament: What project am I willing to plan? What goals can I create to work on now? What employment opportunities am I creating for achievement? How will I be accountable? Who will I be accountable to?

_____

_____

_____

_____

_____

_____

_____

_____

_____

_____

_____

_____

_____

_____

_____

_____

_____

_____

_____

_____

If you don't know who you are, you won't have a grasp on why you are here and what you want to do. If those vital pieces are missing achievement it will be like trying to catch a plane that's already taxiing the runway for takeoff...all you can do is see it. Achievement is guaranteed with purposeful tasks. When you create the goal, you can't complain about the work to be done or choices you have to make in the process, since your initial decision to do created them, too. And no matter how you choose, you will achieve what you chose. So not everything may be easy, but it will be!

Your effort and work ethic correlates with the intensity of the achievement. Achievement happens on the inside (character) and the outside (integrity) easily mirrors and echoes. When athletes train, scientist invent, humanitarians win the Nobel Peace Prize, philanthropists give, musicians win Grammys, actors win Oscars or citizens become kings and presidents – it's all an invigorating achievement that started within and as one goal was achieved, it used the previous one as the stepping-stone and a testament! Those achievements happened internally before they took on an outward role of manifestation. They are a reflection of purpose and proof of the destruction of hindrance. They operated purposefully and strategically. Some great achievers even required an achievement or a self-discovery production team to help them discover that purpose and execute those missions. They weren't ashamed to ask for help, they were so sure of their purpose and knew that their missions were so big it would be epic failure to go it alone. For some reason, a lot of people see asking for help as taboo or a sign of weakness. Weakness doesn't need anybody. Greatness never shows up alone and dreams can't live without plans! You may need help; we all do at some point in time. Acquire an achievement team for your purpose and to promote your life's mission(s)—the bigger, the more teamwork required. Establishing a dream team, a fab five, forming strategic alliances increases the opportunity for you to be your greatest self and cooperate with others, through the investment of purposeful relationships, to have a more powerful and greater reach. Now most of us will never be Olympians or become president. But, your journey of self-discovery will cause your strategies to be award winning and your achievements to be presidential, first to you and then to all you influence, causing a ripple effect on purpose.

Now, you may want to make time to go back to read only what you have written, as this is your experience—it's your testament. You now have an account of this phase of your self-discovery that could very well be one of the most sacred texts you've written or will ever read and implement. It's YOUR testament! It is how you discovered the attributes of God you are here to be and express: your purpose. You may want to take the opportunity to add, change, erase, develop, re-think, rearrange or re-do any of your responses for Your Testament. By all means, feel free to do so! It is the YOU Testament!

Thank you for choosing, reading, asking, answering, implementing, discovering, evolving, creating, benefitting and achieving on purpose.

Peace…

Acknowledgments

I thank God!

I am so grateful for my husband, Owen, and my daughter, Jayda, for their unconditional love and being my greatest cheerleaders and best support team. Macfamily3 for life!

I thank my parents, Walter E. Jones Sr. and Thomasine Rawls Jones, for teaching me spiritual principles, encouraging my discovery, letting me watch their lives through it all, and the freedom to behave accordingly. You are priceless!

Thank you to author Trice Hickman for encouraging me to take this journey into the world of authorship and directing me to the ideal professionals who made the process enjoyable and the outcome successful! Thanks forever, roomie!

Thank you to Jessica Wright Tilles of TWA Solutions and Xpress Yourself Publishing, I greatly appreciate your professional advice, your input for the cover and the excellence in which you carry out your mission—going above and beyond. Kea Taylor of Imagine Photography and Locksie Locks - The Story Tailor, I thank you both for choosing to work with me, accepting book cover idea, my manuscript and for an insightful experience. I learned a great deal from each of you, during this exciting journey. I'm grateful.

I appreciate my family, friends, clients and colleagues who have all been instrumental for the purpose and mission of my life in every way. I love you all. I appreciate wisdom, peace, integrity, abundance, enjoyment, wealth and success for being my purpose and for continuing to successfully guide my life's missions. Absolutely!

About the Author

TracyMac (Tracy McNeil) is a certified life coach helping corporations, non-profit organizations, veterans/dependents, and professional women and men move beyond what may have become mundane or unbalanced—discover, fulfill and continue to achieve their life's purpose and mission. Her brilliant listening skills and intuition facilitate a ripe environment for personal and professional strategic goal achievement and problem solving. She is the ideal go-to for sustaining results and measurable success.

As founder of Peace Place LLC and TracyMac Coaching Services, Coach TracyMac has been coaching since 2004. Serving in many leadership capacities, her twenty-six years of experience include the private sector, non-profits and state and federal government, which gives her the skill to connect with people from diverse cultures and economic levels. She attended Winston Salem State University and later earned her Bachelor of Arts Degree in Behavioral Science from Western International University. She graduated Magna Cum Laude and is a member of the Golden Key International Honor Society. Additionally, she is a graduate of Coach Training Alliance and a Certified Master Life Strategist with Kairos Institute of Personal Discovery.

Her purpose, mission, life experience, sense of humor and heartwarming spirit empowers Coach TracyMac with the ability to assist others in discovering relevant results and practical solutions. Through individual and group coaching, workshops, seminars and keynote speeches, her knowledge and flexibility paves a way to support her clients through their challenges, and she demonstrates the prevailing excellence to help them overcome. She thrives on seeing her clients have breakthrough moments that are life-changing and evident in their success.

Coach TracyMac has proven to be a powerful investment in the success and overall quality of life, by helping others discover, evolve, create, implement and achieve! She invites readers to email her at iamtracymac@live.com, visit her website at www.iamtracymac.com for personal, professional and group coaching, speaking engagements, seminars and workshops. Also, please connect with her on Facebook @ IAMTracyMac and follow her on Twitter @ IAmTracyMac for updates and to receive words of wisdom and encouragement as you live your purpose and continue your journey of self-discovery.

CPSIA information can be obtained
at www.ICGtesting.com
Printed in the USA
BVHW080246130220
572178BV00001B/78